Everyday School Violence

Everyday School Violence

An Educator's Guide to Safer Schools

Sarah E. Daly

ROWMAN & LITTLEFIELD
Lanham • Boulder • New York • London

Published by Rowman & Littlefield
An imprint of The Rowman & Littlefield Publishing Group, Inc.
4501 Forbes Boulevard, Suite 200, Lanham, Maryland 20706
www.rowman.com

Unit A, Whitacre Mews, 26-34 Stannary Street, London SE11 4AB

British Library Cataloguing in Publication Information Available

Library of Congress Cataloging-in-Publication Data

Names: Daly, Sarah E., 1984– author.
Title: Everyday school violence : an educator's guide to safer schools / Sarah E. Daly.
Description: Lanham : Rowman & Littlefield, [2018] | Includes bibliographical references and index.
Identifiers: LCCN 2018020652 (print) | LCCN 2018026738 (ebook) | ISBN 9781475841701 (electronic) | ISBN 9781475841688 (cloth : alk. paper) | ISBN 9781475841695 (pbk. : alk. paper)
Subjects: LCSH: School violence—United States. | School violence—United States—Prevention. | Schools—United States—Safety measures.
Classification: LCC LB3013.32 (ebook) | LCC LB3013.32 .D35 2018 (print) | DDC 371.7/82—dc23
LC record available at https://lccn.loc.gov/2018020652

♾ ™ The paper used in this publication meets the minimum requirements of American National Standard for Information Sciences Permanence of Paper for Printed Library Materials, ANSI/NISO Z39.48-1992.

Printed in the United States of America

Contents

Contents

Foreword

If teachers and students do not feel safe, they will not have the necessary psychological energy for teaching and learning.

—Marzano, 2003

The creation of a safe and orderly climate is a fundamental correlate of an effective school. Unless the climate is free of threats, teachers can't teach, and students won't learn. An educator for over 50 years, I began my career as a high school English teacher, and I worked hard to build a classroom climate of acceptance and willingness to take risks in speaking and writing. My success over 18 years led me to want to extend that environment to the entire experience of high school, the place that students have for years compared to prison. As a high school principal for seven years, I worked relentlessly to craft a climate where *all* students felt respected and cared for, and where teachers received the support they needed to take instructional risks that promote learning success.

I look back on all that experience and conclude that I was really very lucky to have had relatively little violence occur. Lucky, because I used common sense and compassion in my classroom and in my school, but I actually knew very little about school violence! After reading *Everyday School Violence: An Educator's Guide to Safer Schools*, by my former student, Sarah Daly, I find myself wishing I had known much more.

As I reminisce about the school district I was a part of, there was more to the occasional bullying or, less often, fistfights. I continued my educational career as assistant superintendent in a district of four high schools in the Chicago area where, among other duties, I served as hearing officer for the district, the person to whom students could appeal disciplinary rulings and school officials had to make the case for expulsion. I can attest that issues of minor violence have always been a part of any school, regardless of size or socioeconomic status, but violence in today's schools has intensified because of technology and growing incivility. I believe even more strongly that creating an enriching and safe climate for both students and adults is pivotal to academic success and psychological well-being.

As aspiring educators take courses to prepare them to teach or lead effectively, they hope their training will prepare them adequately for what they will deal with in their jobs. As I prepared for the principalship, I took courses in school finance, school law, school leadership, and curriculum design—all intended to prepare me for the challenges I would face, and they did prepare me to some extent. However, I also learned there was much more to the principalship—most pivotally, the climate of the school.

After my retirement in 2000, I came to Saint Mary's College (Notre Dame, Indiana) to teach undergraduate teacher education courses for those who wished to teach at the high school level. I have taught my students, including this book's author (a Spanish major from the University of Notre Dame, across the street), about choosing appropriate assessment techniques, designing thought-provoking units, using cutting-edge instructional techniques, and addressing reading issues across the curriculum. I intended to give them what they needed to obtain and keep a teaching job and, by all accounts, those topics have served them well. However, I am now certain our brief foray into classroom management strategies needed much more time because, while these topics are inherently important to successful teaching and leading, nowhere has the topic of school violence been addressed in such a meaningful way.

Dr. Sarah Daly uses her experience as both a seasoned, successful educator and an insightful researcher into criminal justice to explore violence in school. *Everyday School Violence: An Educator's Guide to Safer Schools* offers readable, feet-on-the-ground insight that is grounded in thorough research. This book is a must read for anyone pursuing a school leadership position.

Furthermore, any newly appointed principal would do well to use this book as a basis for ongoing faculty development as a part of creating a collegial environment to improve student learning. The first three chapters offer a thorough look into the causes and effects of violence, as well as how to create and assess a climate profile for a school. Teachers will benefit greatly from chapter 4's focus on how to create a violence-free classroom by "slowing down the violence." Chapter 5 outlines how leaders can build commitment throughout the learning community, including ways to learn if interventions are working. Finally, the author thoughtfully addresses the issue of school shootings through insight gleaned from her experiences as a criminologist and an educator.

Given the focus on raising achievement over the past 20 years, a great amount of time and money have been spent preparing students for testing and the testing itself, but little attention is given to creating a climate free of threat when teachers are demoralized and students are bored—a potentially deadly combination. This text offers educators a chance to deepen their understanding of violence in its many forms, and provides best practice suggestions for making classrooms and schools safer, healthier, and more positive places to learn.

Dr. Kitty Green
Associate Professor Emerita
Saint Mary's College
Notre Dame, Indiana

Acknowledgments

This book would not have been possible without the incredible people that I have in my life. They offer me support, laughter, and happiness, and I hope they all know every day how much I appreciate their presence in my life.

I came to Saint Vincent College in September 2016, and in the first days after the move, it felt like I moved across the country instead of simply across Pennsylvania. I was initially drawn to the college and the department because of the criminology faculty members, and every day since then, I am assured that I made the right decision. Bruce Antkowiak, our fearless leader, has been supportive of my teaching and research from the beginning. It is an honor every day to come to work in a department that you lead with poise and wit. You have insisted on making me "famous," even if it means waking up early, and I'm thankful for the time and effort that you've spent to further my career. Thank you for everything, Boss.

Eric Kocian is my partner in non-crime on campus, and he, too, has made every day on campus one that is filled with laughter. I respect you immensely; your teaching, your commitment to students, and your dedication to the community is overwhelming. I would surely not have made it through many days were it not for your leaning glances. You have been so helpful in my adjustment to the college, and you have always made me feel welcome in the department.

Sandy Frye is the glue that holds us all together and makes sure that I can even find my way out of my office. Your organization saves my life on a daily basis, and I will take this moment to fully admit that I obviously have no idea how to use a calendar correctly. Thank you for always being happy, optimistic, and fun. I can't say enough how much I appreciate everything that you do.

The students at Saint Vincent College make every day interesting. They are the reason that I wake up and go into the office, and they are often the reason that I'm smiling when I leave. The Criminology, Law and Society Program students (both undergraduate and graduate) remind me that the future of criminal justice is hopeful and bright. So many of my students inspire me. They work hard, they love learning, and they honestly crack me up. It is an honor to teach you all, and I'm lucky to be your professor. A special thanks, too, to my first round of graduate assistants who were always up for work and a challenge. Jonathan, Julie, Felecia, and Kelli, you've been fantastic.

Sarah Jubar and the team at Rowman & Littlefield have been incredibly helpful throughout this process. You have been patient, kind, and informative, and it has been a joy to work with you.

This book is intended to be an homage to educators, and I have known amazing ones. Dr. Kitty Green in the Department of Education at St. Mary's College got me excited about teaching. Dr. Stevenson, Dr. Dupree, and Dr. Thomas at the University of Pennsylvania, and Dr. Humphries and Dr. Siegel at Rutgers University–Camden shined the light toward the doctoral program and instilled in me a love of research. Dr. Samuels and Dr. Boxer at Rutgers University–Newark served on my dissertation committee, with Dr. Sullivan at the helm, initially studying school violence with me for months before focusing on mass shootings.

I received an education at many different institutions, but I learned everything I know at Camden County Technical School. I experienced the good and the bad, I laughed and I cried, and I carried every experience and every story with me. The students there are still the reason that I study schools. The success stories—along with the ones that didn't end well—remind me every day that there is work to be done. This is for Carey and ShaPaul, whose stories ended tragically, and for Jamal and Lamar, who defied the odds.

The employees at CCTS are some of the most outstanding people I have ever known. Their grit and determination are worthy of a medal, and I'm sure there's a group photo of us all that will eventually be placed next to the definition of "resilience." In the face of adversity (and often, absurdity), they laugh, they work, and they keep fighting for the kids. Janice, Ritzius, Jamie, Trabosh, Shelly, Doug, Christian, Amy, Eva, Brett, Holly, and more are the reason that I wrote this book. They are many of the teachers whose stories I share, and they are brilliant educators.

And of course, I can't write anything without explaining how I have always managed to grin and bear it. Leigh and Cory are always the next adventure that gives me something to look forward to. My angels, this is wonderful. Thanks for letting me bless you. My Notre Dame friends, Ricky, Laski, Lindsay, and Delaney are perfection as usual. Alex S. doesn't fit into a group, so she gets her own sentence and appreciation for being a person.

I said that this book is an homage to educators and that it wouldn't have been possible without my friends. It is only fitting that I end with a thank you to my mom, Marie Daly. She is a consummate educator and counselor. I learned so much from her, and she's my best friend to boot. Thank you for always being my loudest cheerleader, my biggest fan, and my hero.

Introduction

Schools across the United States are grappling with issues of safety and security. In a time when school shootings make headlines and threats are commonplace, everyone is demanding answers and action. Mass shootings and violent incidents highlight what many have known for years: when students are afraid, the learning environment suffers. And while many parents and students have been acutely aware of school violence in the years since Columbine (and due to school shootings even before 1999), other communities have experienced fear in schools for decades before that, and on a daily basis.

Common school violence often gets pushed to the back burner in the aftermath of extraordinary violence, but for those who attend and work in schools with fistfights, weapon carrying, and overall disorder, the problems are real, daunting, and exhausting. Students may be fearful on the commute to and from school, while teachers may hesitate to intervene in a fistfight due to fear of personal injury or a lawsuit.

While this may be foreign to some readers, others may be all too familiar with these feelings. Perhaps most troubling are the long-term effects of everyday school violence. Children who engage in violence in schools are more likely to drop out of school, enter adulthood exhibiting signs of aggression, and have contact with the criminal justice system (NAACP Legal Defense and Educational Fund, 2008).

Schools are tasked with educating students, but they are similarly expected to develop and grow children into upstanding citizens. Yet, when obstacles like poverty, special needs, mass incarceration, hunger, mental illness, gangs, and more hinder progress, the goals of education seem unattainable. Combined with increasing demands and expectations of schools and school employees, it is hard to know where to begin, especially when there is no one-size-fits-all solution.

First and foremost, this book is designed to help educators and, therefore, help children. By combining research and experience, the goal is to offer suggestions, best practices, and resources to the individual reader as well as institutions. Additionally, this book combines educational approaches with psychological and criminological approaches.

While these three fields often function as three unrelated disciplines, there is more overlap than most realize. From studies in aggression to development to the school-to-prison pipeline, it is hard to ignore the interconnectedness of the three subjects; we must use a more holistic approach to understanding violence and, more importantly, how to reduce and prevent it.

Chapter 1 offers an overview of aggression and violence. To understand why students are violent or why they misbehave, it may be helpful to examine criminological theories to serve as a structural foundation for later work. The chapter offers multiple theories, because you may have your own beliefs and feel that one theory explains your school's problems better than others. In scholarly works, academics insist that theory drives research, which in turn should influence policy. This should certainly be the case in practice, and this chapter is an attempt to begin the process in a quick, readable way.

Chapter 2 provides a discussion about measuring violence, problems with conducting school violence research, and methods for assessing violence in your own school. By providing a crash course in research methodology in the context of school violence, the hope is that the chapter will start your thinking about how your own school assesses violence and how the data can drive effective changes and programs. Additionally, the examples of school studies as well as baseline data for national violence trends can serve as roadmaps for your own ideas.

Chapter 3 aims to examine the short- and long-term effects of violence and the ways in which schools and communities are often stuck in cycles of violence. In the midst of violence, teacher disengagement and fear, high turnover, and harsh punishment, schools often want to change but are at a loss for how to do so. By revisiting the consequences of fear, violence, and punitive measures, this chapter serves as a reminder that change is necessary to save children and make schools safer.

Chapter 4 is for individual readers to reflect on their own experiences and think about how they respond (or would respond) to violence in their own school. It provides seven steps for prevention and de-escalation that may be simple to implement, but also may have profound effects on violence and student fear. It also encourages you to think about your own role in physical violence and asks you to think about what to do (and perhaps more importantly, what not to do). Violence typically occurs in an instant, and it becomes a split-second decision. By "slowing down the violence," school employees are given a chance to think and prepare before an incident occurs.

Chapter 5 is written more for administrators, safety officers, and teachers or faculty who seek a leadership position. By convening a school safety committee and using a step-by-step process to create evidence-based, data-driven programs and policies, schools can create their own approaches to school safety. Following these steps allows for a committee to create goals and objectives, use data to measure effectiveness, and evaluate and adapt to make improvements.

Unfortunately, in the weeks before this manuscript was completed, the nation was horrified by the attack at Marjory Stoneman Douglas High School in Parkland, Florida. While this book initially set out to address issues of more common, everyday school violence, I would be remiss if I did not address the issue and offer insight and recommendations in the midst of a nationwide debate on school safety and gun violence.

In sum, the book offers best practices, but also takes into account the fact that schools and school employees are under-resourced and overwhelmed. At the very least, there may be pieces of the text that you find useful or helpful. Many of you will already know this information, as it comes from years of experience and training. It may be more useful to newer teachers, so that they might fast-track their own hands-on learning. Know, however, that wherever you are in your career and whatever you hope to do, the work that you do now is incredible, honorable, and often underappreciated.

In all that you do, and as you read, consider how local resources including police, colleges and universities, and nonprofit organizations might fit into these steps and offer support to you and your students. Whatever you choose to take from this book, though, know that you are appreciated, and that the burden to protect schools and students is not yours to bear alone. We are in a time that demands action, change, and progress; the consequences are dire.

This book may not provide all the answers, but it starts with the tools that you need to create programs designed specifically for your school, because it is your students whose safety and futures hang in the balance. As Dennis Gabor wrote, "The future cannot be predicted, but futures can be invented" (Gabor, 1963). High school students from Florida are leading the charge for change, and this is the time for that change, so that we can look to the future with a positive, hopeful goal of safer schools for every child.

Chapter One

An Overview of Aggression and Violence

How much more grievous are the consequences of anger than the causes of it.
—Marcus Aurelius

Those who work in schools typically spend much of their time addressing the onslaught of problems that arise each day. For teachers, lesson plans, grading, tutoring, and teaching take up most their time. Administrators evaluate teachers, attend meetings, dole out discipline for wayward students, and tend to budgetary and administrative needs.

The list of responsibilities for all school employees seems endless. Those charged with the great responsibility of educating the future of America bear the brunt of meeting the requirements and expectations that federal and state leaders, politicians, and parents throw at them. Amid budget crises, increased standardized test expectations, and more, school employees are underappreciated, unsung heroes. They are the people who get things done, who make sacrifices, who work tirelessly every day to ensure a brighter future for students.

Academics and researchers face different challenges. Those who devote their careers to training future teachers and school leaders must balance teaching strategies, technology, and pedagogy while also preparing young educators for the everyday challenges they will face. Education graduates arm themselves with knowledge, enthusiasm, and tactics before they step into their classrooms, prepared to teach their first class. Researchers examine the efficacy of strategies, develop new techniques, and try to empirically measure theories, policies, and relationships so that those in the field might use them to improve outcomes.

Perhaps what differentiates academics from practitioners most is the focus on theory. Ask any educator in a violent school why some students fight, and she will give you an accurate answer: parents, poverty, hormones, drama, stress, and more. In theory and in practice, these responses certainly explain aggression and violence.

Take, for example, a fistfight between two students. Those who know and teach the students may understand why they engaged in violence. They may know about their tumultuous home lives or prior instances of emotional instability. However, the most typical school response to this is punishment, most commonly in the form of a suspension.

The students may be required to sit with a counselor upon their return to school, and a principal might call their parents, but for the most part, the theoretical underpinnings of the problem remained unaddressed. In the flurry of real-world dilemmas and real problems that need immediate answers, the theory often takes a backseat to a reasonable, quick, and seemingly effective solution.

Similarly, educators are realistic and understand that poverty is often a strong correlate of violence, though they may not consider the mechanisms by which it occurs. Academics study the effects of poverty on criminality, development, learning, and behavior. Yet, walking through this logic, if families, communities, and schools had more money and better resources, violence would disappear. Though this is a heartwarming idea, practitioners understand that this is unlikely, and academics may lobby for increased funding and social programs.

Academics in education, criminology, psychology, and sociology may think about and study violence, but they are often incredibly far removed from the schools, communities, and environments in which violence and poverty occur. These two groups—academics and researchers—exist simultaneously, fighting for what they believe to be right, with a common goal of helping children. One group works on the ground, while the other works in the academic "ivory tower," but the two rarely come together to solve problems in a long-term, meaningful way.

This is certainly not an indictment or criticism of school employees or researchers, as both have their place in society (and share the goal of helping and educating), but rather an example to highlight the differences in how academics and practitioners examine and address problems. This chapter uses criminological theories to reframe issues of aggression in children and teenagers. Some may seem obvious, while others may reframe or organize ideas in a new way. They do, however, offer a foundation for policy and programs.

To quash the problems for good and to address them at their core rather than applying quick fixes, schools and academics need to create alliances and partnerships to develop theory- and evidence-based policies and programs designed to prevent and effectively respond to school violence.

Thus, the purpose of this chapter is to offer criminological theory, not to simply speculate about the root causes of the problem, but to use theories of deviance, aggression, and criminality to create ways to address the issues in schools. By pairing these with school employees' knowledge and experience of students and schools, these theories become the foundation of the solution. They serve as a critical background for readers continuing through the book, as they are to be used in conjunction with prevention programs and ideas.

The next section offers a discussion of adolescent development in terms of neurology and brain development, as well as psychology. Unlike theories that inform policy, this root-cause description essentially aims to provide a context in which to think about adolescent behavior and development, and understand why teenage behavior may be so frustrating and inexplicable at times.

ADOLESCENT DEVELOPMENT: THE BRAIN, PSYCHOLOGY, AND SOCIALIZATION

Modern scientific studies have concluded that the brain is not fully developed until age 25 (Casey, Getz, & Galvan, 2008; Giedd et al., 1999; Reiss, Abrams, Singer, Ross, & Denckla, 1996). For adolescents, this underdevelopment in the prefrontal cortex and myelination affects impulsivity and risk-taking, vulnerability to peer pressure, and less rational behavior. [1]

In their *amici curiae* argument in the *Roper v. Simmons* (2005) U.S. Supreme Court decision to abolish the death penalty for crimes committed by juveniles, the American Psychological Association (APA) wrote, "Scientists have documented the difference [between adolescents and adults] along several dimensions. Adolescents as a group . . . are more impulsive than adults. They underestimate risks and overvalue short-term benefits. They are more susceptible to stress, more emotionally volatile, and less capable of controlling their emotions than adults" (p. 2). Thus, in the context of schools, peers, and social situations, teenagers and preteens may need to work harder than school employees realize to maintain self-control and make good decisions. Students are less future-oriented, and often fail to consider the long-term consequences of their actions (Cauffman & Steinberg, 2000; Furby & Beyth-Marom, 1992).

This research certainly does not imply that students who engage in violence are not responsible for their actions, but rather considers identifying potential explanations for youth violence. It helps to explain the moments in which school employees are dumbfounded by their students' lack of responsibility or self-control. These studies and conclusions also offer insight about why prevention and intervention models created by adults may not be effective for juveniles. Educators often craft programs and strategies that seem as though they would logically work for them, but they may fail to consider that adolescents are not necessarily wired in the same way that adults are (and thus require a different approach).

To gain a more thorough understanding of adolescents in the context of brain development and schools, school employees can also utilize a psychological approach. The fundamentals of psychology highlight the ABCs (and additionally, the Ds and Es). The ABCs represent affect, behavior, and cognition. Understanding a student's feelings, actions, and thought processes, respectively, can remind teachers and school employees that teenagers function at a fundamentally different level than do adults. While higher-order, mature processes are always the goal, it may be beyond the scope of ability for some students.

Further complicating the issue are the Ds and Es of psychology: desires and environment. Though some students may seem goal-driven and future-oriented, others may be more impulsive and seek short-term rewards. For these students, their desires may look much different, and their affect, behavior, and cognition would reflect that.

Moreover, the environment (particularly a school setting) is unique for students in that it becomes a social stage. Educators aim to make the school a second home of sorts, offering education, support, and services, but for many students school is a place that may be the source of anxiety, fear, or pressure. Adults who work in a school often tend to view it from their own perspective with their own struggles, friend groups, and obstacles. The affect, behaviors, and cognition of the students in the school, however, occur in the context of this environment and essentially serve the purpose of either achieving their desires or avoiding unwanted stimuli.

Peers serve as a fundamental part of the school environment, especially given the importance of social behavior and relationships during adolescence. Elkind (1967) developed his notion of the "imaginary audience" when explaining adolescent egocentrism. He describes the phenomenon as the teenager constantly believing that he is the focus of everyone's attention. As Elkind (1967) notes, "Since he fails to differentiate between what others are thinking about and his own mental preoccupations, he assumes that other people are as obsessed with his behavior and appearance as he is himself. *It is this belief that others are preoccupied with his appearance and behavior that constitutes the egocentrism of the adolescent*" (p. 1029, italics in original). This, in turn, affects self-consciousness and self-esteem as well as affect, behavior, and cognition.

The most ironic, if not depressing, notion of the imaginary audience is that each student in a school is an actor in his own story while also the audience for others. Such complicated, performed interactions with students require them to consistently act in a way that they expect and know that their peers will scrutinize.

In the context of social media, this explains why today's teenagers feel the need to take 72 selfies before identifying the best one to post on six different outlets. In the context of school violence, it explains why students may feel the need to defend their honor or garner respect in a public way by using physical aggression, relational aggression, and retaliation.

Elkind (1967) also identified and defined the term "personal fable" as the reason why students often refuse to listen to reason and advice from adults. Like the imaginary audience, this mental construction provides a developmental, psychological explanation of how and why adolescents may be so impulsive, stubborn, and egocentric. Because he is the star of his own show in front of this imaginary audience every day, he becomes rather self-centered and unwilling to consider other perspectives, even from adults who have likely experienced the same trials and tribulations of adolescence.

Elkind (1967) describes this as a "personal uniqueness" and humorously (and accurately) states, "Perhaps because he believes he is of importance to so many people, the imaginary audience, he comes to regard himself, and particularly his feelings, as something special and unique. Only he can suffer with such agonized intensity, or experience such exquisite rapture" (p. 1031). For many teenagers, their own struggles are the worst that have ever happened, their crushes are the greatest love stories ever told, and their actions are not irresponsible, for they will never experience the consequences of them.

Vartanian (2000) also notes that both the imaginary audience and the personal fable aid in the development of identity and psychological separation from their parents. She asserts that "Emphasizing feelings of uniqueness, omnipotence, and invulnerability (i.e., engaging in personal fable ideation) helps the adolescent to conceive of the self individualistically, that is, apart from family ties" (p. 647).

Newer literature has focused on the "new look" theory, which builds upon Elkind's (1967) two mental constructs and examines how identity development occurs in teenagers and adolescence. Modern academics assert the need for more empirical tests of both personal fable and imaginary audience, but as a preliminary framework for understanding school violence and young egocentrism, the two constructs are useful tools in gaining perspective.

When you consider the neurological development of children and teenagers, particularly in the context of psychological and moral development, it becomes easier to remember why adolescents often engage in the behaviors that they do. Schools may have certain expectations of behavior and conduct, and those students who can achieve them are typically successful.

As Kohlberg (1968) noted, "If a child throws back a few adult clichés and behaves himself, more parents . . . think that the child has adopted or internalized the appropriate parental standards" (p. 27). Schools and educators, too, may adopt the same train of thought, but they need to continue to consider behavior in the context of environment, psychology, and neurology and accept that moral, acceptable behavior is a journey that may be more difficult for some than others. While it may be profoundly frustrating to educators whose life work is to guide students toward a path of success and away from poor choices, student behavior may make more sense by using this biopsychosocial framework of thinking about the issue.

CRIMINOLOGICAL THEORY: NOT JUST FOR CRIMINOLOGISTS

The previous section focused on biological and psychological development to understand adolescence as a unique time in life, but this section presents criminological theories as the basis for understanding deviant or delinquent behavior in schools and for crafting policy and programs to address violence.

Criminology as a discipline is relatively young and still unable to identify one simple explanation for why crime occurs. Throughout its history, criminology has attempted to create theories and explain criminality, deviance, and essentially "why crime occurs." As Cullen and Agnew (2011) note, "beyond the development of ideas *within each theoretical perspective* . . . there is also the issue of when different schools of thought first came on the scene and/or became major influences within criminology" p. (5).

While there are a number of perspectives and theories in the field, this chapter aims to offer four of the most prevalent: deterrence, strain, social bond, and differential association. There may be similar features to them, but they differ in terms of practical applications.

The paragraphs that follows offer a basic overview of the tenets or propositions of each theory, its relationship to school violence, and a discussion of its shortcomings in school practices. As you read, choose a theory that you believe most clearly applies to the student population and community you serve (or, quite simply, the one you agree with the most). Later chapters will offer the process by which theory and practice come together, but this chapter provides structured explanations of the theories of aggression and violence in schools.

Deterrence Theory

The premise of deterrence theory is a simple one: people do not commit crimes because they don't want to face the punishment if they get caught. It is the original Hobbesian notion that punishment for the crime must outweigh the benefit that comes from committing it in order to prevent an individual from engaging in the criminal act.

First published in 1764, Cesare Beccaria's *An Essay on Crimes and Punishments* laid the groundwork for classical criminology. Rooted in Hobbesian belief that "people naturally pursue their own interests and . . . this pursuit of self-interest frequently leads people to harm one another" (Cullen & Agnew, 2011, p. 22), Beccaria argued that there should be certain elements to punishment in order to make it an effective deterrent. The primary features of punishment should be swiftness, severity, and certainty.

First, the punishment must occur as quickly as possible in order to create a relationship between a negative behavior and the consequence. Delays, for whatever reason, make the punishment less effective. Beccaria (1764) wrote, "the smaller the interval of time between the punishment and the crime, the stronger and more lasting will be the association of the two ideas of *Crime and Punishment*; so that they may be considered, one as the cause, and the other as the unavoidable and necessary effect" (p. 74).

Second, the punishment must be in proportion to the crime. Beccaria argued that the consequences of the crime should be severe enough to deter the individual from committing the act, but not so harsh as to create an unjust society or to encourage other, lesser crimes. More importantly, though, was the third idea of certainty; Beccaria (1764) wrote, "Crimes are more effectually prevented by the *certainty*, than the *severity* of punishment. . . . The certainty of a small punishment will make a stronger impression, than the fear of one more severe, if attended with the hopes of escaping" (pp. 93–94).

Deterrence can have two forms: general and specific. General deterrence is intended for the larger population to prevent crime. Punishment of other offenders—incarceration or the death penalty, for example—serves as a deterrent for the rest of the population who have not committed crimes.

Specific deterrence, though, focuses on individuals. This is targeted at a specific person in order to prevent him—and him alone—from committing another crime. In the criminal justice system, the most common form is probation. Probationers are fully aware of the specific, individual consequences that they will face if they are to violate the terms of their probation or commit another crime.

Lawmakers generally craft policies, laws, and sanctions for the purpose of general and specific deterrence in order to keep the public safe. School administrators do the same. Students are punished not only for rehabilitative or retributive purposes, but also to serve as an example so that other students are inspired to follow the rules in order to avoid consequences. Schools often go to great lengths to make consequences for negative behaviors known to students.

If, for example, students are to engage in a fistfight, they may face a lengthy suspension or criminal charges. Using general deterrence theory, the motivating idea is that students will heed the message and choose to consider the consequences before fighting. For some students, this may be effective in preventing violence. Students may realize that the punishment is severe, acknowledge that it may have long-term effects on their future, and look to courses of action other than fighting.

However, using the biological and psychological framework in the previous section, it seems that deterrence theory may fall short in terms of reducing or preventing violence in the ways that school administrators hope. Adults tend to be more averse to risk. Think, for instance, why you would choose to avoid a bar fight if possible. You might get hurt, you might seriously hurt someone else, and your job would be in jeopardy if you faced criminal charges.

Teenagers and adolescents, however, are armed with a brain that has not fully developed; their own personal fable and imaginary audience; and a reputation to protect among their peers. Under these circumstances, they may believe that the punishment is not harsh enough to outweigh the benefits. They may not even stop to consider the consequences at all before running into a fight with fists blazing and temper flaring.

Given the findings about teenage impulsivity, lack of awareness, and emotional volatility, the latter seems much more likely. If you ask most students what they were thinking about before throwing the first punch, they will likely tell you "I wasn't thinking at all," or "I just knew what I had to do," indicating that the deterrence that educators hope will prevent violence does not serve that purpose in the heat of the moment.

Deterrence theory does still certainly play a role, especially for more mature, logical students who are generally well-behaved. However, in order to effectively use deterrence theory as the foundation for a policy or program in a school, it must be coupled with other evidence-based practices for anger management, cognitive behavioral therapy, or more specific deterrence for at-risk students.

Strain Theory

Strain theory is one of the most easily understood and widely cited theories of criminal behavior. Classic strain theory, developed first in the 1930s by Robert Merton, focused on two specific types of theories. The first part of the theory, "anomie," speaks to the institutional, macro-level, highlighting the ways in which society and culture focus on widely accepted goals and the ways in which these goals are achieved. When society emphasizes the goals without providing appropriate means of acquiring them (for a variety of reasons), society is said to be in a "state of anomie." In such a state, individuals are forced to use the easiest means of achieving the goals, including criminal behavior.

The second part of the theory focuses on "strain." If anomie is a state of society or an institutional characteristic, strain is the individual manifestation of those conditions. Agnew (2006) explained that there are three specific types of strain. Strain arises from negative relationships in which others "(1) prevent or threaten to prevent the achievement of positively valued goals (e.g., monetary success, popularity with peers), (2) remove or threaten to remove positively valued stimuli (e.g., the loss of a romantic partner, the death of a parent), or (3) present or threaten to present negatively valued stimuli (e.g., insults, physical assault)" (p. 45).

According to Merton (1938), some people are typically more apt to engage in criminal behavior because they are blocked from achieving success through legal means and experience more negative relationships as a result of poverty, lack of education, and more. While there are varying levels of strain, he argues that strain contributes to crime by increasing negative emotions, affecting levels of social control, and reducing the ability to cope with stressors.

A student of Merton, Albert Cohen (1955), expanded on this work and focused specifically on the role of schools in developing strain and anomic conditions. Cohen wrote specifically about delinquent boys in gangs, and he argued that a delinquent, lower- and working-class subculture forms as a result of the inability to achieve middle-class goals. He found that schools in particular create a unique problem for those students who come from families with less social and economic capital. Schools, by and large, were (and still are) filled with educators who are typically considered middle class. Thus, they judge academic and behavioral success by middle-class standards, which Cohen (1955) called "the middle-class measuring rod" (p. 84).

Cohen noted that teachers and administrators may perpetuate middle-class ideas through a variety of expectations for their students. Such expectations include ambition, ethic, self-control, manners, controlling aggression, and respect. While they may have seemed to be educationally and developmentally appropriate goals for children, those who fell behind or were not up to par (as measured by the middle-class measuring rod) may have been considered troublesome and received harsh discipline in order to instill them.

When such students fail to achieve these goals, "one solution is for individuals who share such problems to gravitate toward one another and jointly establish new norms, new criteria of status which define as meritorious the characteristics they *do* possess, the kinds of conducts of which they *are* capable" (Cohen, 1955, p. 66). By disavowing their commitment to middle-class standards, they recommit themselves to a group in which they can find success and their perceived shortcomings (like aggression) are hailed as positive.

More than 60 years later, these problems persist. The income and achievement gaps continue to grow, and minority students are subject to harsher discipline compared to their white peers (Baker, Farrie, & Sciarra, 2016; Burke, 2011; NAACP Legal Defense and Education Fund, 2008).

Educators still struggle to find the line between teaching students to be global citizens and punishing those who fail to meet the expectations as defined by the middle-class measuring rod. While there are heartwarming, motivational stories, there are still hundreds and thousands of children who fall through the cracks and find their way into a successful delinquent subculture when they cannot or do not reach the socially accepted goals of the school environment.

Programs focused on strain theory aim to make students more comfortable in the school environment by setting individualized goals for them, rewarding small successes, and minimizing strains when possible. If students are able to find opportunity for achievement and success in school (by using a variety of different measures), they may be less inclined to look to a deviant subculture to thrive.

Social Learning and Differential Association Theory

Social learning theories posit that children learn crime, attitudes, and deviant behaviors from others. Psychologist Albert Bandura (1977) found that children learn aggression through observation and imitation. Children in the experimental group watched a video of an adult acting aggressively with a blow-up clown doll (affectionately named "Bobo") by punching, throwing, and hitting the doll with a hammer. Compared to the children in the control group and the group who watched a nonaggressive video, the children in the experimental group acted more aggressively toward the doll. This experiment paved the way for discussions about media violence, transmission of social behaviors, and observational learning.

However, before Bandura's Bobo doll experiment, Sutherland and Cressey (1960) set forth their differential association theory and asserted that individuals learn criminal behavior through their social interactions. These interactions, or associations, are important as they can vary in intimacy, thus affecting the degree to which the messages are transmitted and learning occurs. They explained that delinquency occurs when there is an excess of "definitions" that are favorable to violating the law as compared to definitions unfavorable to violating the law. These definitions are shared, taught, and learned through social interactions and intimate personal groups.

While others in an individual's social network may be sharing definitions unfavorable to law violations (e.g., teachers encouraging students to engage in academics, pastors preaching about nonviolence, and parents enforcing rule-abiding behavior), a child may be more inclined to heed messages from his close friend group. These differential associations (or competing, counteracting groups and messages) vary in frequency, duration, priority, and intensity. If the messages or definitions are shared for longer periods of time and more frequently, they are more likely to remain with the child and outweigh other definitions communicated in fewer interactions. Additionally, priority refers to the weight that an individual places on the person sharing the message, while intensity refers to the importance and force of the message.

The differentiation of the competing forces and the varying measures of the communication of these definitions seem to explain why the opinions and advice of teachers and parents may take a backseat to those of an adolescent's peers. As teenagers struggle for identity and independence, they often look to their friend groups and peers for support and guidance. As a result, their opinions (and thus, their delinquency and definitions favorable to crime) may take precedence over what they used to know was wrong. Studies have frequently found that delinquent peers are the strongest predictor of crime (Gordon et al., 2004; Warr, 1998; Thornberry, Lizotte, Krohn, Farnworth, & Jang, 1994).

In schools and neighborhoods, differential association theory manifests itself through groups of troublesome students sharing ideas and definitions. As Sutherland and Cressey (1960) explain, "In an area where the delinquency rate is high, a boy who is sociable, gregarious, active and athletic, is very likely to come in contact with other boys in the neighborhoods, learn delinquent behavior from them, and become a gangster" (p. 77).

Sutherland and Cressey's original theory provided the foundation for social learning theory. His eighth proposition asserted that the learning of criminal behaviors and definitions occurs in the same way as all other learning. While likely accurate, he does not explain the processes or mechanisms by which this learning occurs.

To expand on and complement these ideas, Akers (1998) developed a model of social structure and social learning (SSSL). In this model, he outlined the four specific groups of social structural factors—social organization, location in the social structure, structural variables, and social location in groups—which in turn affect differential association. In addition to differential association, there are factors that affect social learning, including imitation, differential reinforcement, and other learning variables.

Akers (1998) explains, "The social structural variables are indicators of the primary distal macro-level and meso-level causes of crime, while the social learning variables reflect the primary proximate causes of criminal behavior that mediate the relationship between social structure and crime rates" (p. 322). In the context of schools, this essentially means that factors such as social class, race, population density, social disorganization, peers, and family affect the interactions in which a child is able to learn these definitions (favorable and unfavorable toward crime) while learning it in various ways through differential association, differential reinforcement, and imitation. In schools that serve high-poverty, at-risk communities, the likelihood of finding definitions favorable to crime may be greater due to risk factors and opportunities for criminality.

Creating a program rooted in differential association and social learning theories would require changes in the reinforcement and associations while offering increased opportunities for positive imitation and interactions with those who may take priority in the child's life. Doing so may increase the number of definitions unfavorable toward law violations and encourage conforming behavior.

Social Bond Theory

Criminologists tend to classify theories into different time periods or central themes, such as learning or classical theories, as discussed earlier. The final theory in this chapter addresses the group known as control theories. This set of theories examines the mechanisms through which individuals engage in specific behaviors through the development of neutralization theories (finding ways to neutralize the controls of morality and conformity), containment theories (controls presented by stable external mechanisms like family, neighborhood, and society), and self-control theory (parental influences shaping children by teaching them boundaries and control).

The last of the control theories (though third, chronologically), social bond theory, is of particular importance when considering youth violence, as it posits that the quality and meaning of relationships formed in institutions like schools affect their decisions to engage in crime. While relationships with parents are paramount, other influences can also affect delinquency. Hirschi (1969) argued that the four elements of these relationships and institutions are attachment, commitment, involvement, and belief.

First, *attachment* relates to the level in which an individual connects to another person or people. Attachment translates to the notion that the quality or importance of a positive relationship (and maintaining it) would overtake the urge to engage in delinquency. Parents (and other meaningful adult relationships, such as mentors or teachers) can be direct or indirect controls in a child's life, given their varying levels of attachment.

Direct control involves clear supervision, but for adolescents and teenagers who spend more time away from their parents, indirect control plays a more important role. Stronger levels of attachment create indirect control such that teens considering their parents' opinions, concerns, and beliefs before engaging in (or ultimately, avoiding) delinquent or negative behavior.

Commitment speaks more to the institution or rewards that are related to the individual. For example, teenagers can commit themselves to school by studying and taking advantage of educational opportunities in order to succeed. As Hirschi (1969) notes, "The idea . . . is that the person invests time, energy, himself, in a certain line of activity—say, getting an education. . . .

When or whenever he considers deviant behavior, he must consider the costs of this deviant behavior, the risk he runs of losing the investment he has made in conventional labor" (p. 218). If students feel more committed to the institution of school and the conformity to conventional goals (which they will lose if they are caught engaging in delinquent behavior), they are less likely to violate rules and law for fear of wasting their hard work and energy.

Involvement refers to the activities in which an individual participates or time commitments that an individual makes. This notion is often the underpinning for after-school activities, as students who are spending extra hours at the school are not on the streets committing crimes or interacting with delinquent peers. Increased involvement in extracurricular activities, church groups, part-time jobs, or babysitting siblings do not leave opportunities for juveniles to engage in delinquency. Hirschi (1969) applied the notion of "idle hands are the devil's workshop" and noted that "the leisure of the adolescent produces a set of values, which, in turn, leads to delinquency" (p. 220).

Finally, *belief* refers to the extent to which the individual believes that he should obey the rules. While Sutherland and Cressey's theory focused on definitions about committing crime, beliefs refer specifically to laws and rules. Thus, the absence of beliefs about conformity and abiding by rules set forth by the governing body results in crime. As Hirschi (1969) states, "there is variation in the extent to which people believe they should obey the rules of society, and, furthermore, that the less a person believes he should obey the rules, the more likely he is to violate them" (p. 221).

Similarly, psychologist Tom Tyler (1992) argues that people are more likely to obey the law if they feel that the laws are legitimate and that legal authorities use fair and just procedures to enforce them. In schools, these notions of belief and legitimacy should be reinforced and supported by school employees and administrators. In the context of legitimacy, their role is to help students to understand why certain rules are in place and ensure that students believe that the rules are important, fair, and meaningful for the greater good of the school.

OTHER NOTIONS

While these are some of the foremost criminology theories that can be applied to schools, there are other studies in sociology, psychology, and criminology that address other variables in youth violence, delinquency, and school behavior. These may not be complete theories that can explain crime (or the absence of it) or outline the mechanisms or processes as the other theories, but research has shown the positive effects of hope and resilience among adolescents. Further, the following sections aim to serve as an inspiration, a ray of positivity, and a reminder that there is purpose and meaning in your profession as an educator.

Hope

While many studies focus on risk factors for crime and delinquency, others study protective factors such as social support groups, social bonds, and parental monitoring. Another, often understudied, factor is hope. Children who come of age in poverty and violent communities may experience feelings of hopelessness. As DuRant, Cadenhead, Pendergrast, Slavens, & Linder (1994) found, African American urban youth were more likely to believe that they would not live until their 25th birthday.

As Hirschi (1969) noted, if children have committed themselves to their future success or goals, they are more likely to avoid delinquent behaviors. However, if at-risk children believe that they have bleak or nonexistent futures, they may be more inclined to engage in risky or delinquent behavior as opposed to engaging in activities that will prepare them for successful adulthood.

By its dictionary definition, hope is the feeling or desire for a certain event to occur. In the literature on development and delinquency, it is a cognitive construct or motivational skill that can mediate effects of witnessing or experiencing violence. Cedeno, Elias, Kelly, and Chu (2010) conducted a study in which they investigated "the psychological and behavioral impact of school-based violence and the influence of hope in low-income, African American, elementary-aged children" (p. 214). As the researchers defined it, hope is "a goal-oriented, iterative cognitive process comprise of *agency* and *pathways* thinking" (p. 215). Pathways thinking refers to the mind-set of creating plans and processes by which a child can achieve goals, especially in the face of an obstacle or problem. Agency is the belief and motivation that he or she can, in fact, pursue those goals. Using these two methods of measuring hope, the researchers found that "hope moderated the effects of personal victimization and witnessing violence" (p. 222). Moreover, girls who felt higher levels of hope experienced higher levels of self-concept, particularly at higher levels of experienced or witnessed violence.

While the broad notion of hope may not necessarily lend itself to a school-based program, utilizing the notions of pathways thinking and agency may lead to programs that aim to teach at-risk youth about problem-solving, self-esteem, and planning for the future.

Resilience

Along the same lines as the hope research, Henderson and Millstein (2003) define resilience as "the capacity to spring back . . . rebound, successfully adapt in the face of adversity, and develop social and academic competence despite exposure to severe stress" (p. 7). Intrinsic, personal characteristics that contribute to internal resilience are self-esteem, self-efficacy, agency, and self-control. External resiliency are outside influences that enhance a child's ability to bounce back, such as supportive parents, positive friends, and attachment to social groups or institutions.

Woodland (2016) explains that a child or youth is considered resilient when two conditions are present: "(a) exposure to substantial risk, trauma, and/or severe adversity, and (b) the achievement of positive adaptation despite major risks and/or adversity" (p. 771). He asserts that after-school programs can promote resiliency among at-risk black urban youth by reducing vulnerability and risks, reducing stressors, increasing available resources, mobilizing protective processes, and utilizing culture as an asset. In doing so, these goals can teach children to overcome trauma and risk while also strengthening community and family ties in order to create more stable support systems for children who need it most.

Hinduja and Patchin (2017) measured resilience by asking middle and high school students to use a Likert scale to respond to statements like "I am able to adapt when changes occur" and "I am easily discouraged by failure" (p. 54). They found that higher levels of resilience served as a protective factor for students against bullying. Those who had higher levels of resilience were less likely to be bullied in school or experience cyberbullying. Not only were they less likely to be victimized by their peers, but higher levels of resilience mitigated the effects of bullying.

CONCLUSION

This purpose of this chapter was to provide an overview of the myriad theories available to explain youth aggression, delinquency, and violence. Though they may be somewhat contradictory or may be best suited in conjunction with other theories, they present the framework for thinking about aggression as you move through this book. Eventually, when the time comes to develop a program or policy, it should without a doubt be rooted in theory and empirically tested ideas. Using these or other theories as building blocks for effecting change allows school employees and administrators to alter the most influential and important variables that affect school violence.

NOTE

1. For more information about brain development in context, see Romer, Reyna, & Satterthwaite (2017).

Chapter Two

Measuring School Violence

Statistics is the grammar of science.

—Karl Pearson

Few would disagree that violence in schools is a nationwide problem. From increasing concerns about bullying to mass shootings, there is little doubt that students today face many potential conflicts that affect their learning, development, and general well-being. However, when attempting to quantify the issues and identify the exact scope and frequency of the problem, there may be a number of challenges for people who wish to examine school violence.

How can you, as a school employee, know exactly which problem to address if you do not understand the number of students affected or the severity of the issue? Teachers and other employees are often acutely aware of the unique problems that exist in their own schools, but they may be frustrated by the lack of interest or concern from those who implement or enforce policies. Schools and school employees can use data and descriptive statistics to focus on the problems and highlight their concerns.

In these instances, it may be helpful to supplement your own knowledge and experience, not only with national data, but also school-level data that can quantitatively emphasize the exact points you are attempting to make. It may be easy for someone to ignore a teacher's concern that students feel scared at school, but if that teacher presents survey data from students showing that nearly one in three students at the school are fearful, it suddenly becomes a more pressing issue.

This chapter begins with a summary of the difficulties that arise when studying issues of school violence, and offers ways that school administrators can address the issues. It continues by providing a variety of organizations and datasets that are available for understanding a number of school violence issues. It shares a crash course in research methodology so that school employees who are interested in collecting data may have a starting place to begin in their own institutions. Finally, the chapter also presents statistics about the nationwide prevalence of school safety issues and demonstrates how such information can be utilized in school-level studies.

THE CHALLENGES OF STUDYING VIOLENCE

From a young age, children learn about the scientific method. They understand that they start with a problem or a question, create a hypothesis, and test the hypothesis in a controlled scientific way. Researchers in the social sciences—including psychologists, criminologists, and sociologists—examine social problems in the same way, although there can be a number of challenges with such research.

Many experiments are conducted outside of a controlled lab, and therefore affect the ways in which scientists can interpret data. Further, attempting to find trends, patterns, and relationships among the millions of teachers, students, and school employees is a daunting task. Though not impossible, it is sometimes difficult for even the most skilled researchers to find efficient, methodologically sound ways to measure school violence, identify predictors and risk factors, and create ways to address the issues.

Researchers face five main challenges when studying school violence, ranging from methodological issues to issues of access. Without getting too complicated with research methodology, this section offers a brief description of the obstacles and ways that school employees and administrators can address them in their own work and when collaborating with researchers.

Generalizability

In most instances, it is impossible to survey every person in a population. For example, we hope to understand how many students in this country are affected by school violence, but it would not be efficient, cost-effective, or reasonable to contact every student in the United States. Rather, researchers rely on sampling to provide a representation of the larger population.

As an example, the National Crime and Victimization Survey (NCVS) uses a systematic method of random sampling to contact households and interview all members of those households (provided they are 12 years of age or older).[1] The researchers interviewed nearly 50,000 households and more than 70,000 individuals; their findings are hugely helpful in understanding rates of victimization across the United States. While the survey is not administered to everyone in the country, it provides a stronger picture of reported and unreported crimes.

The NCVS also includes a School Crime Supplement (SCS) and asks respondents about their experiences with and perceptions of school crime and behavior. Although this is only for students ages 12 and older, it still provides a large-scale sample of students nationwide. Other national measures of school violence include the Youth Risk Behavior Survey (sponsored by the Center for Disease Control), the Schools and Staffing Survey, the School Survey on Crime and Safety, and the Early Childhood Longitudinal Survey. These massive yet important undertakings are valuable for providing findings and research from national surveys.

The large sample sizes and advanced methodology allow for generalizability, so that the random nature of some sampling can make the finding applicable to the population that the sample represents. However, there are limitations to aggregate data. A summary of the nationwide problem may not necessarily apply to individual schools and communities. For example, the NCVS SCS found that "Between 2001 and 2015, the percentage of students ages 12–18 who reported that gangs were present at their school decreased from 20 to 11 percent" (Musu-Gillette, Zhang, Wang, Zhang, & Oudekerk, 2017, p. 64).

It is helpful to conclude that 11 percent of students in the United States report a gang presence, but this may not shed light on cities and schools in which a gang presence or gang-related activity is higher. Using the same nationwide survey but examining the disaggregated data, researchers found, "In 2015, a higher percentage of students from urban areas (15 percent) reported a gang presence at their school than students from . . . rural areas (4 percent)" (Musu-Gillette, Zhang, Wang, Zhang, & Oudekerk, 2017, p. 64).

However, in a Consortium of Chicago School Research (CCSR) study, *Student and Teacher Safety in Chicago Public Schools* (Steinberg, Allensworth, and Johnson, 2011), researchers found that 63 percent of teachers related gang activity to either "some" or "to great extent" of the crime and disorder in their school. In the same study, there were even differences in reported school safety issues between schools in the same district despite the fact that they served similar student populations. In this sense, we must examine the ways that we use national data and surveys and the extent to which the findings are generalizable, especially to schools with unique circumstances and problems.

To address this, school employees and administrators can use this data (both aggregated and disaggregated) as a starting point to which they can compare their own data. When they engage in a problem analysis and survey of their own students or teachers, they may find that the problem is more pronounced or more prevalent than the nationwide representations.

The national data can offer methodologically sound survey measures and serve as a barometer, but schools need to remember that their own approaches and programs should reflect the individual needs of the students and schools that they will serve.

Conceptualization and Operationalization

In addition to issues of generalizability, there is another issue in school violence research that creates problems for researchers. "Conceptualization" and "operationalization" refer to the ways in which we outline, define, and measure the terms that we use to talk about school violence.

As an example, a group of teachers, faculty members, and administrators may choose to tackle the issue of school violence, but what exactly does school violence mean? Will they be examining risk factors and safety measures to protect from school shootings? Or will they be discussing the number of fights and reports of bullying in the last year? Speaking of bullying, what does that mean, and what definition is used? To ensure that everyone has the same understanding of the problem and a uniform way of measuring it, we must conceptualize and operationalize the terms.

Conceptualization requires you to create a definition that clearly explains the parameters of the problem you are attempting to study. For some, the notion of verbal disrespect toward teachers may not necessarily be considered violence, but for others, it may be an integral piece of understanding the larger culture of school violence. If you were to begin with a Google search of school violence, you would find news results and commentary about school shootings, discussions about metal detectors and zero tolerance policies in schools, statistics about nationwide school crime rates and their relationship to national crime rates, and fact sheets that offer yearly rates of student deaths at school.

This is all relevant to the initial search, but it may also be information overload and make it hard to discern where to begin with the problem. Because the term "school violence" is so broad, it is difficult to narrow down the results list and find useful information. By conceptualizing your own terms, you will be able to narrow your search terms, filter the results, and utilize research and facts that are more relevant to your specific school's problem.

Even when the terms are clearly defined, studies and articles that focus on the same topic may not use the same means to measure the problems. Operationalization involves creating measurement tools or means for quantifying the conceptual terms. To demonstrate differences in operationalization methods, we look at the previously mentioned 2011 Chicago Public Schools study and the 2008 Virginia High School Safety Study (VHSSS 2008).

The Chicago study conceptualizes the notion of student-teacher relationships as "Whether students feel their teachers care about their learning and overall well-being" and "Whether students feel safe with and listened to by their teachers" (Steinberg et al., 2011, p. 36). Table 2.1 offers a comparison of the two survey measurements tools. Both are measuring the conceptual notion of teacher-student relationships, but they measure them through differing sets of questions and scales.

While some of the questions may be similar, there are also subtle differences in the ways that the questions are phrased and the nuances of the sentences. The Virginia study seems to ask questions about the teacher collective, whereas the Chicago study speaks directly to the individual teacher in the classroom where the participant is completing the survey. The Virginia study also speaks to the students' perceptions of teachers' aspirations for their students. The difference in the scale measurements and the subtle differences in the questions may make it a bit difficult (though not impossible) to compare the findings between the two studies.

Table 2.2 shows the difference in definitions of student victimization between the Virginia study and the NCVS SCS. This example eloquently highlights differences in the conceptualization of "student victimization" and the way this would, in turn, affect operationalization and measurement.

Note the differences in the level of detail that each of the definitions provide. The NCVS SCS offers more specific differentiations between varying types of victimization, while the Virginia study uses a broader, more generic operationalization. Both are certainly acceptable, but in making sense of the statistics that each study presents, it is imperative that readers understand the ways in which violence and victimization are conceptualized and operationalized. Further, observing these methods allows you to understand

Table 2.1. Operationalization of Student-Teacher Relationships

Chicago Study (2011)	Virginia Study (2008)
Measured by Strongly Disagree, Disagree, Agree, and Strongly Agree	Measured by Disagree/Strongly Disagree, Somewhat Agree, and Agree/Strongly Agree
• My teachers always keep his/her [sic] promises.	How much do you agree that the adults in the school . . .
• My teachers always try to be fair.	• Really care about all students.
• I feel safe and comfortable with my teachers at this school.	• Acknowledge and pay attention to all students.
• When my teachers tell me not to do something, I know he/she has a good reason.	• Want all students to do their best.
• My teachers will always listen to students' ideas.	• Listen to what students have to say.
• My teachers treat me with respect.	• Believe that every student can be a success.
• My teachers really care about me.	• Treat all students fairly.
• The teacher for this class really cares about me.	• Support and treat students with respect.
	• Feel a responsibility to improve the school.

Table 2.2.   Varying Conceptualizations of "Student Victimization"

NCVS SCS (2016)	Virginia Study (2008)
"'Total victimization' includes theft and violent victimization. 'Theft' includes attempted and completed purse-snatching, completed pickpocketing, and all attempted and completed threats, with the exception of motor vehicle thefts. Theft does not include robbery, which involves the threat or use of force and is classified as a violent crime. 'Serious violent victimization' includes the crimes of rape, sexual assault, robbery, and aggravated assault. 'Violent victimization' includes the serious violence crimes as well as simple assault. 'At school' includes in the school building, on school property, on a school bus, and, from 2001 onward, going to and from school."	"Student victimization (various forms of victimization ranging from personal theft to being threatened, bullied, or assaulted; perceptions that there is a lot [of] teasing and bullying at school, presence of gangs at school)."

the ways in which you should define and measure your own variables and concepts when you define and evaluate the program in your own school.

The Virginia study researchers operationalized their conceptual definition by asking students if they had experienced damage or theft to personal property worth more than $10, been physically attacked, received obscene remarks or threats, or had a weapon pulled on them. Then they compared those results and examined the correlations between school size, percent of students on free or reduced lunch (as a measure of poverty), and the percentage of nonwhite students. As you can see, the operational definitions related directly to the conceptualization, and are the means through which the concept is measured.

For your conceptualization, be sure that concepts such as school violence, victimization, and bullying have clearly defined parameters, including specific indicators or examples. These conceptualizations should explain the concept while also providing clarity about the inclusion and exclusion criteria by which you will evaluate the problem. The operationalization should offer the means to measure the specific problem and include the scale or tools. In the example in Table 2.1, the Chicago and Virginia studies both clearly provide the scales used to evaluate each indicator or element of the concept, and they illuminate the various components that make up the definition.

Causality

In research, there are a variety of types of studies that one can conduct. The first, exploratory research, focuses on larger ideas and seeks to understand the scope of the problem and provide background information. Such research typically examines problems that have not been studied or have been relatively understudied.

Exploratory research often serves as the basis for future descriptive and explanatory studies by providing an overview of the problem. The goal of this type of research is to determine if the proposed problem is, in fact, a problem. The findings from this type of research can serve as the basis to create more detailed questions and identify variables that should be studied in descriptive research. Though it often lacks formal research methodology, it offers the opportunity to identify relevant factors and environmental issues in the school environment.

Descriptive research, however, provides systematic statistical representations, which again provides information and understanding. More importantly, though, it uses basic quantitative measures like mean, range, and median to provide a mathematical representation of the variables learned about in an exploratory study. It is more structured than exploratory research, as it answers questions such as "Who does this affect?" and offers basic information about the scope and frequency of the problem. The question that it does not answer, however, is "Why?"

Explanatory research aims to answer the question "Why?" by focusing on causal relationships. By identifying links and relationships between variables that pertain to specific outcomes (the independent and dependent variables), this type of research is valuable because it uses highly structured statistical models to identify the level of influence on the behaviors you will examine. Essentially, explanatory research asks, "What are the causes of the problem, and what level of influence do they have?"

In order to prove causality (or, stated differently, a cause-and-effect relationship between two or more variables), there must be three criteria. When designing an explanatory study, you first need to prove that there is chronological order between the variables in question and the outcomes. This is also known as temporal precedence.

As an example, can you prove that there was an ongoing beef between gang members before you began to see an increase in physical conflicts on campus? Or, while there may be a correlation between teacher attitudes and negative student behaviors, can you prove which came first? The second example is a prime demonstration of the phrase "correlation does not equal causation." Do negative teacher attitudes cause the negative student behaviors, or do the negative student behaviors lead to negative teacher attitudes?

In order to measure this, you would need to create questions that attempt to answer these questions to prove temporal precedence.

Next, you must note that there is an existing relationship between two or more variables, and that they have a cause-and-effect relationship. In methodological terms, this is known as covariance of cause and effect. Using prior research or empirical evidence, you can highlight that there has been a clear relationship in the past between variables like poverty, academic achievement, aggression, and negative school climates. In order to prove that one (or more) variables directly causes or influences another, you must indicate not only that there is a known relationship, but also that as one variable changes, so, too, does the other.

Finally, you must demonstrate that there is no better explanation provided by other variables. By eliminating other extraneous variables, you highlight the clear relationship between the variables you are examining and acknowledge that there are no other possible reasons for the expected outcome. If you cannot do this, you run the risk of allowing competing ideas or influences to explain the dependent variable. This would distort your findings. You want your results to be as clear as possible.

When teaching about the importance of causality in criminal justice methodology courses, professors often use the ice cream sales and homicide example. While there is a clear correlation between the two, it lacks causality. First, there is the absence of any existing relationship between ice cream and murder. Eating or purchasing ice cream does not lead an individual to homicidal behavior, nor does murder generally lead to an increased desire to buy or consume ice cream.

This also indicates that there is no temporal relationship between the two. Most importantly, though, the extraneous variable here is warm weather. It is well documented in the crime literature that homicide rates spike in summer months and so, too, do ice cream sales.

As such, it becomes important for you to note the influences of other factors on your dependent variable(s), to highlight the temporal order of your variables, and to search for the pre-existing relationships between the variables that you are evaluating.

Consent

Perhaps one of the most difficult aspects of school violence research is gaining access. Schools are notoriously hesitant to allow researchers into their facilities for any number of reasons. Larger cities tend to have their own offices to address research requests, and they often form partnerships with local colleges and universities. Even then, access to students can be difficult.

First and foremost, ethical research practices demand that all subjects involved in research receive proper information about the study. Children are known as a protected population, so their participation in studies is under increased scrutiny by Institutional Review Boards, an entity designed specifically for this purpose. Children (and students) under the age of 18 not only need to affirm their own informed consent, but they also need the consent of a parent or guardian. Rather than simply walking into a school and distributing a survey or conducting an interview, a research team needs to provide forms for parents or guardians to sign and wait for these to be returned before conducting any research.

Schools who conduct their own research for school purposes may not need to gain any such permission, but a partnership with a college or university for research purposes would require it. However, even in a perfect world where this consent is relatively easy to achieve, it is often difficult to find time to conduct research. Surveys and interviews take time, and when schools are constantly rushing to meet new (and old) demands, administrators and teachers tend to avoid measures that would take away from instructional time.

As such, when designing research studies of all types (descriptive, exploratory, etc.), you must consider the amount of time that the measures will take. Even then, you need to be sure that the benefits of the project or the study are worth the time that they require. As such, it helps to keep brevity and concise language and structure in mind as you create instruments for surveys, interviews, and focus groups. There should be a balance between the conservation of time and thoroughness in collecting data and addressing the problem.

Self-Reporting Problems

Finally, there is the issue of the actual questions. Of particular importance are the ways in which questions are asked and who, exactly, is doing the asking. The primary problem is the honesty in responding. The perceptions and experiences of teachers and students may be affected by relationships and feelings about administrators and those who administer the test. Self-reporting issues may arise in survey research, interviews, and focus groups, and the data obtained are different than concrete data such as discipline reports or incident reporting.

Anonymity and confidentiality can assist in ensuring that responses are honest, although in cases of interviews and focus groups, it may be more difficult to promise that participant identities are protected. If the researcher knows the respondents or has a position of authority over them, it may influence their responses. A well-liked administrator, for example, may elicit kinder or more tempered answers from the subjects. Or, depending on her demeanor and reputation, she may actually receive more honest answers than would another administrator who has a history of being vindictive or less trustworthy.

When speaking with or surveying students, their own perceptions of the tester or researcher may similarly affect their answers. If, however, they do not know the researcher but are assured that their answers will be protected (and that no one will be able to link their responses to their identities), they are more likely to be honest. When possible, utilizing outside personnel (such as university or college partners, or people in the school who are less well known to the respondents) may be helpful.

Finally, questions should be worded clearly and in such a way that they are concise and understandable. They should be developmentally appropriate for the subjects, and the questions and responses should leave little room for interpretation. They should be straightforward, offer clarity about words that could have multiple connotations, and be specific. The beauty of designing research, however, is that no one is asking you to reinvent the wheel here. Rather, you can refer to other studies and questions that have been used to address the problems that you believe are specific to your school. Examples of questions and surveys are available through a number of organizations, agencies, and institutions. Such data are available online and can offer questions that you, too, can use in your own research. More importantly, you can use these resources as baseline data to which you can compare your own results. For example, if 45 percent of student respondents reported theft in school, and your own results are actually higher, then this may be an issue worthy of consideration.

Examples of surveys and sample questions include the Bureau of Justice Statistics' Indicators of School Crime and Safety (published yearly). This includes a number of questions and data from multiple sources, including the NCVS School Crime Supplement, the School Associated Violent Death Surveillance System, the Fast Response Survey, and the National Center for Education Statistics.

There are also studies available from state and private sources, such as the previously mentioned Virginia High School Safety Study and the *Student and Teacher Safety in Chicago Public Schools* study.

In addition to providing valuable data and methodology that can often be replicated in your own school, they also provide examples of the conceptualization and operationalization of the variables and questions that were used in the survey. The Virginia High School Safety Study also offers a clear outline of the questions used, in addition to the sources for each of the measures.

For example, the study explains that for measures of student support, it uses three different scales including help-seeking, learning/working environment, and encouragement of help-seeking, and provides the three separate studies that it used for each. For help-seeking, the Virginia researchers explain that it is a "6-item scale from the School Climate Bullying Survey (Cornell & Sheras, 2003) designed to measure teacher perceptions of student willingness to seek help from school staff members for bullying and threats of violence" (VHSSS, 2008, p. 24).

THE STATISTICS

This section of the chapter offers an overview of the school violence statistics. These can provide a baseline for understanding the issues in the aggregate and comparing your own school environment to the national statistics. It also provides insight, as previously noted, about the types of questions that researchers and educators can ask to discern the scope and frequency of the problem in question.

Overall, school violence researchers tend to note that children and students are often safer at school than they are away from it. With the rare exception of school shootings (to be discussed in chapter 6), children are incredibly unlikely to die at school. In 2005, the *Indicators of School Crime and Safety* found that youths are 70 times more likely to be the victims of homicide away from school than in school (DeVoe, Peter, Noonan, Snyder, & Baum, 2005).

Further, Mateu-Gelabert and Lune (2003) found that 33 percent of student fights involved some kind of carryover between neighborhoods and the school; 18 percent began in school and went to a neighborhood, whereas 21 percent began in a neighborhood and were brought to the school. Such findings serve as a reminder of "the effect of the school and neighborhood structures on adolescent violence, [and] that school violence is a highly contextual and dynamic process" (Mateu-Gelabert & Lune, 2003, p. 353).

Keeping this in mind when reviewing rates of victimization, it is also important to note the difference between aggregated and disaggregated data. First, the national rates of victimization are important because they provide baseline data for examining patterns and trends over time. Additionally, schools can compare their own rates using similar definitions and scales. The 2016 *Indicators of Crime and School Safety* report (Musu-Gillette et al., 2016) noted that the overall victimization rate was 33 per 1,000 students at school. This represents a steady decrease since 1992, when an astonishing 181 victimizations per 1,000 students was reported. However, the rate of victimizations does not necessarily offer a very clear picture of what this looks like in schools across the country. Instead, it becomes helpful to disaggregate the data and start to examine it in terms of the types of crimes and victimizations, in addition to the characteristics of the victims.

Figure 2.1 shows aggregated and disaggregated victimization rates and compares them to victimizations at school and away from school, using NCVS data.

Examining the data as a larger picture (total victimization) and in terms of theft and serious violent victimization provides a better picture of the scope and type of problem. While theft is certainly a problem in schools that needs to be addressed, it helps to know that victimization of theft is more common than serious violent victimization, and this fact provides direction and guidance that agencies, organizations, and schools can use.

Similarly, when considering issues of school violence, it is, as noted previously, important to conceptualize the issues. School violence can also

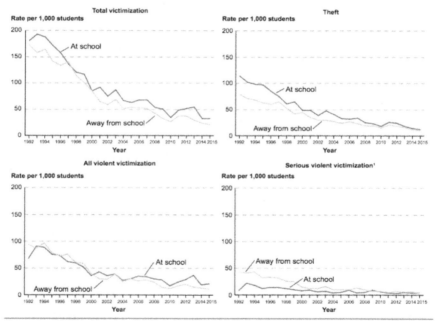

[1] Serious violent victimization is also included in all violent victimization.
NOTE: Due to methodological changes, use caution when comparing 2006 estimates to other years. "Serious violent victimization" includes the crimes of rape, sexual assault, robbery, and aggravated assault. "All violent victimization" includes serious violent crimes as well as simple assault. "Theft" includes attempted and completed purse-snatching, completed pickpocketing, and all attempted and completed thefts, with the exception of motor vehicle thefts. Theft does not include robbery, which involves the threat or use of force and is classified as a violent crime. "Total victimization" includes thefts and violent crimes. "At school" includes inside the school building, on school property, and on the way to or from school. Although Indicators 2 and 3 present information on similar topics, Indicator 2 is based solely on data collected in National Crime Victimization Survey (NCVS), whereas Indicator 3 is based on data collected in the School Crime Supplement (SCS) to the NCVS as well as demographic data collected in the NCVS. Indicator 2 uses data from all students ages 12–18 who responded to the NCVS, while Indicator 3 uses data from all students ages 12–18 who responded to both the NCVS and the SCS. Inclusion criteria for the NCVS and SCS differ slightly. For example, students who are exclusively homeschooled are able to complete the NCVS but not the SCS. The population size for students ages 12–18 was 25,581,700 in 2015. Detail may not sum to totals due to rounding. Estimates may vary from previously published reports.

Figure 2.1.   Indicator 2: Incidence of victimization at school and away from school. *2016 Indicators of Crime and School Safety document, available at https://nces.ed.gov/pubs2017/2017064.pdf*

be measured in terms of disorder, perceptions of fear, harassment, fights, gang presence in schools, threats, and even death on campus. The disaggregated data are important to understanding the specific types of issues that schools and students face, while also examining the problem in the larger context.

Even more, disaggregated data help to understand how these problems affect specific groups of students. You can disaggregate data based on age and grade, race and ethnicity, socioeconomic status, school setting, and gender. Such a nuanced approach with descriptive statistics provides a better picture of the students who are experiencing violence and victimization, and can also provide a clearer picture of the groups and how they may experience school differently than others.

As an example, for students in grades 9–12 who reported being threatened or injured with a weapon on school property at least once in the previous 12 months, the percentages were higher for black and Hispanic students (7.9 and 6.6 percent, respectively) compared to the 4.9 percent of white students who reported threats. Similarly, a lower percentage of female students reported being threatened or injured on school property compared to male students.

Such disaggregated data can help identify discrepancies, over-representation of certain groups (compared to their proportions as respondents), and groups that should be more clearly targeted for intervention and prevention techniques. These disaggregation strategies can also be helpful in your own analyses and research.

Referring back to the Chicago and Virginia safety studies, the questions and categories can be incredibly useful as you attempt to understand and measure specific problems in your own schools. The Virginia study specifically notes measures of school structure, student support efforts, student engagement, student victimization, and teacher victimization. By asking both teachers and students for the first two measures, the researchers were able to capture and compare responses while generating important descriptive data. As the researchers noted, "There was modest agreement between ninth-grade students and teachers in their perceptions of the school rules" (VHSSS, 2008, p. 6), but they noted the discrepancies between awareness of zero tolerance policies and the importance of perceptions of respondents.

Their study is important, though, in that it created a methodologically sound research study that can be used to highlight important differences and concerns among high schools in Virginia. Further, their use of pre-existing surveys and variables that are already conceptualized and operationalized can assist you in creating a tool that is useful, valid, and meaningful for future interventions and policies.

The Virginia study also found important (though relatively unsurprising) findings in terms of perceptions of school climate associated with school size, poverty, and minority status. For example, schools with more low-income students "perceived less fairness in how rules are enforced and less supports from adults in the school. . . . They were more likely to report being bullied or physically attacked, and having personal property stolen" (VHSSS, 2008, p. 7). They also found that "students in schools with more minority students were less likely to express willingness to seek help for bullying . . . and for a threat of violence" (p. 7).

At the school level, victimization rates were higher in schools with gangs, but lower in schools with stricter dress codes, higher teacher support of students, higher administrative support of teachers, and higher daily structure. These findings highlight the correlation (but not the causation) between these variables, but descriptive statistics like these can be the beginning of a discussion about victimization, perceptions, and school safety and frame a similar project for your own school or district.

The Chicago study also examined student and teacher perceptions of safety in addition to measuring student perceptions of peer interactions. In addition, the researchers included demographic data, state exam scores, U.S. Census blocks, neighborhood crime rates, and qualitative data. The qualitative piece is important in that the researchers conducted in-depth, semi-structured interviews with 72 students and made observations in two high schools.

The qualitative data allowed for typological analysis and case study observations like "respectful interactions with students keep conflicts manageable" and "an uninviting reception makes it difficult for parents to be partners" (Steinberg et al., 2011, pp. 39–40). By providing detailed conclusions drawn from observations of interactions and environments, the researchers are able to paint a descriptive, more vibrant picture than quantitative data may offer.

As one case study outlines, "In the worst cases, sarcastic remarks and thinly veiled insults pass in both directions between students and teachers at Lake Erie. Both adults and children are sensitive to the threat of losing face in front of one another" (Steinberg et al., 2011, p. 40). The stories that follow detail interactions that support this notion, allowing the reader to imagine the scene rather than calculating the numbers of quantitative data. Such in-depth detail often provides a human element to research, too.

In another case study, the researchers assert that suspensions can make students feel unsafe. This has been largely documented in similar research and through the use of surveys, but the observational notes offer insight on the interactions among an administrator, a teacher, and her students, allowing the reader to see a situation in which this may be the case. Student statements such as "they be suspending people for no reason" and "the hallways get crowded . . . then you'll miss your class . . . even if you were trying to run to class, you'll get suspended" (Steinberg et al., 2011, p. 35) provide a narrative to the researchers' assertions and make the students' voices real to the reader rather than simply providing numbers and figures.

CONCLUSION

Research design and data analysis often bring back nightmares of painful college courses, but they can be immensely helpful when examining issues of school violence. By acknowledging difficulties and challenges in measuring school safety problems, school administrators and educators can tackle the problems head on, work to create methodologically sound research and practices, and identify ways in which new and existing data can be used to create school-specific, tailored programs and policies.

Also, it bears repeating that these challenges are not ones that schools must address alone. College and universities are often seeking to create partnerships with school to engage in community partnerships, and education (or psychology or criminology) departments may be willing to conduct research studies and collaborate with schools in mutually beneficial partnerships. Academics and researchers are trained in research methodology, and are often eager to find ways to help students and school districts.

Finally, national data, including the yearly *Indicators of School Crime and Safety* report, may serve as an important resource for schools. Individual schools and districts can use the measures as baseline indicators to which they can compare their own rates of violence and victimization. In doing so, they can identify areas in need of improvement and aspects of safety and security that are above average.

Moving from the concrete statistics, it becomes necessary to think about what these rates and frequencies truly mean both in the present day and for the future. The next chapter outlines the current research on the effects of violence in schools on students, teachers, and the school environment.

NOTE

1. https://www.bjs.gov

Chapter Three

The Effects of Violence

I object to violence because when it appears to do good, the good is only temporary; the evil it does is permanent.

—Mahatma Gandhi

With each new school shooting, the public often revisits the notion of fear at school. Parents fear what may happen to their children at school, students fear that they may be next, and teachers reconsider the benefits of their job compared to the fear of potentially dying at work. These are certainly valid concerns, and ones that must drive future discussions about violence in schools. How do fear and perceptions of safety affect learning and the school environment?

Researchers have long studied this idea, and there is a clear relationship between perceptions of fear or victimization and academic problems. Not only do widely publicized school shootings affect the school experience, but so, too, do violent learning environments in which assaults, threats, and thefts are commonplace.

This chapter examines the individual effects on students, teachers, and schools. It also identifies larger effects on learning and the community. In addition, the chapter aims to review the problems with punitive measures used to address violence, and how they may actually have adverse effects. It concludes with a discussion of effective ways to balance safety and perceptions of fear.

INDIVIDUAL EFFECTS ON STUDENTS

Though violent crime has decreased substantially since its peak rates in the 1990s, students may still experience fear of targeted violence and now, in light of recent tragedies, the fear of large-scale, random violence perpetrated against schools, such as the attack in Parkland, Florida. The likelihood of serious injury or death at school is markedly higher away from school than at school, but *perceptions* of danger and safety are as important (if not more so) than the reality. As Bosworth, Ford, and Hernandaz (2011) note, "Perceptions of school safety may or may not correlate with concrete safety statistics. . . . Yet recent school safety studies have shown that perceptions of school safety may have greater influences on students than do the concrete incidents measured by statistics" (p. 195). If students feel unsafe at school, they may experience negative consequences or outcomes that can adversely affect their school experience.

EMOTIONAL, BEHAVIORAL, AND ACADEMIC PROBLEMS

Researchers and educators have long known that children cannot learn when their basic needs are not met. Clearly, students need food, water, and shelter to thrive, but safety is also an important piece of Maslow's hierarchy of needs. With bullying in the forefront of school safety discussions, there is little doubt that it is a pervasive problem among school-age children.

Vidourek, King, and Merianos (2016) found that nearly 30 percent of students participating in the School Crime and Safety Survey reported being bullied in the past year, most often in a stairwell or in a classroom. The authors note that "Students who were bullied were approximately six times more likely to report fear at school and six times more likely to report school avoidance than students who were not bullied" (p. 126). Students have also reported avoiding specific class locations in school due to fear. Similarly, Wang and Holcombe (2010) found that disruptive or poor behavior can lead to frustration, boredom, and disinterest in students, while Beane, Miller, and Spurling (2008) found that programs to address school safety and reduce bullying and violence positively affect attendance rates.

Aggression and violence not only negatively affect all the students in school, but also those who perpetrate it. Kupersmidt and Coie (1990) found that aggressive students and those who were rejected by their peers are at substantial risk for later disorder, including dropping out and police contact. They also found that excessive absenteeism (due to fear or other factors) is also a significant predictor for dropping out of school. For students who are absent from school due to suspensions for aggression or due to fear of bullying or threats to personal safety, avoidant behavior obviously has negative impacts on future academic success.

Further, Akiba (2010) found that low academic achievement and a weak sense of student belonging at school were the strongest predictors of students' fear. Other relationships between variables included classroom disorder and lower levels of teaching-student bonding as well as mean parental education. The Chicago Consortium (Steinberg, Allensworth, & Johnson, 2011) found that "Students who are victims of harassment attend school less frequently and feel less connected to and engaged in school" (p. 7).

Overall, it is clear that perceptions of fear and safety can be influenced by any number of factors, but the effects can be long term and far reaching. These perceptions can affect students' sense of well-being, their behavior, and their academic and personal outcomes. Most research, though, has consistently found that positive relationships with teachers and school employees can affect student engagement and mediate the negative effects of fear.

When using this information to survey your own students, it may be helpful to use perceptions of fear and safety as dependent variables. While you may have access to concrete data such as discipline reports and statistics about violence, student and staff perceptions may capture the problems more accurately and identify factors that affect their feelings in school. Given the consistent research findings about the effects of fear, it becomes important to use this as a measure of your own school's issues and ways to address fear.

GENDER DIFFERENCES

While there is some disagreement among researchers about gender effects, more studies have found that girls are more likely to experience fear at school than boys. In addition to a greater likelihood of previous physical or sexual victimization (which would affect their perceptions of safety), girls are also more likely to perpetrate and be victims of relational aggression, which includes exclusion from social activities, damaging reputations, or withdrawing attention and friendship. Such behavior could affect feelings of safety or danger while at school, even in the absence of physical violence.

EFFECTS ON TEACHERS

While the school violence studies often focus on school climate and student safety, the safety of teachers and school employees is another element to consider. While adults in school are less likely to be victimized or experience violence, there is still the possibility of danger, either from a current student at the school or from an intruder. School disorganization, violence, and student misbehavior can have short- and long-term effects on school employees, and those effects can, in turn, influence the school and the students.

In the *Indicators of School Crime and Safety* document (Musu-Gillette, Zhang, Wang, Zhang, & Oudekerk, 2017), indicator 5 measures the rates for teachers threatened with injury or physically attacked by students. Using data from the Schools and Staffing Survey (SASS), the researchers found that during the 2011–2012 school year, "9 percent of school teachers reported being threatened with injury by a student from their school" (50). While this is lower than the percentage who reported threats in 1993–1994, it is still higher than other academic years since then.

Additionally, the researchers found that "The percentage of teachers reporting that they had been physically attacked by a student from their school in 2011–2012 (5 percent) was higher than in any previous survey year" (50). Further, while there were no gender differences between teachers who had been threatened with injury, 6 percent of female teachers reported being physically attacked by a student compared to 4 percent of male teachers. In the Chicago Consortium study, the researchers found that at one Chicago school, "three-quarters of teachers reported that students threaten them with violence" (p. 15).

While threats and physical attacks are clearly alarming, they are still relatively rare among respondents. However, in one of the largest studies to date of teacher victimization, the American Psychological Association Task Force on Violence Directed Against Teachers (Espelage et al., 2013) surveyed nearly 3,000 K–12 teachers about their victimization experiences in the current or past year. The task force found that 72.5 percent of teachers had experienced at least one incident of harassment, 50 percent had experienced property offenses (e.g., theft), and 44 percent reported physical attacks. While this is starkly different than the Schools and Staffing Survey results, it presents interesting findings and offers a new perspective on violence against teachers.

In addition to observing and being the victims of verbal mistreatment and threats, teachers and other adults in schools may also experience high levels of stress as a result of student misbehavior and threats. A 2004 French study of more than 6,000 teachers found that "a feeling of insecurity at school was the dimension of school climate which is most predictive of teacher burnout" (as cited in Galand, Lacocq, & Philippot, 2007).[1] Victimization in schools as a feeling of insecurity can lead to negative emotions and workplace functioning. In a review, Espelage et al. (2013) found that "the general teacher research literature indicates that job related stress can lead to dissatisfaction with the profession for teachers and lowered commitments to the profession" (p. 77).

Using structural equation modeling, Galand et al. (2007) surveyed teachers to measure school support, school violence, well-being, and disengagement. They found that incidents of school violence (as measured by students' misbehavior, perceived violence, and verbal victimization) were related to school support and well-being. Negative well-being was related to somatization, depression, and anxiety, which affected disengagement.

More importantly, though, the authors found that "school support plays a key role in the risk of exposure to school violence" (Galand et al., 2007, p.

473). While teachers may experience negative consequences because of exposure to school violence and victimization, strong supports in school through colleagues and leadership can affect well-being. The authors even found that the total effects (both direct and indirect) of school support are greater than the direct effect of school violence. This research provides justification and support for the notion that teamwork, collegiality, and supportive administrators can provide positive interactions for teachers (and other employees), even in the face of violence and school disorder.

Bosworth et al. (2011) found that faculty members "cited relationships (e.g., the faculty respects students, the faculty cares, 'we're like a family'), climate, and physical characteristics (e.g., small size, proximity to danger) as key factors that help make a school safe" (p. 197). As Espelage et al. (2013) note, "teachers who are well equipped with evidence-based techniques to mitigate and manage potentially violent behaviors may experience not only an enhanced sense of empowerment but reduced levels of job-related stress" (p. 77).

ISSUES OF PUNISHMENT

In recent years, many school districts have focused on more punitive measures to address issues of violence and student misconduct. Given the ongoing downward trend in school violence incidents, it is somewhat concerning that rates of suspensions have been steadily increasing since the mid-1970s.

Like general crime rates, the public tends to believe that common school violence is increasing despite the fact that rates are actually decreasing. Not only does this affect academic outcomes for students who misbehave (in often common, typical adolescent ways), but it can contribute to the school-to-prison pipeline, negatively affect social bonds with the school, and enhance issues of discriminatory treatment of minority students.

The School-to-Prison Pipeline

Punitive measures can include in-school suspension, out-of-school suspension, and expulsion for behaviors that may have been addressed in alternative ways in past decades. However, with increasing concern for school violence and misbehavior, many schools choose to use harsher punishment as a general deterrent for their student bodies. By implementing such policies, the idea is to dissuade students from engaging in these behaviors, although the notion itself may be contrary to the impulsive nature of the teenage brain. Given the challenges of adolescence discussed previously, zero tolerance policies may not have the same deterrent effect that they would have on fully developed adults.

Zero tolerance policies were originally developed and implemented in schools to address problematic behavior such as drug use, weapon carrying, or violence. The American Psychological Association Zero Tolerance Task Force (2008) notes that

> the term became widely adopted in the schools in the early 1990s as a philoso-phy or policy that mandates the application of predetermined consequences, most often severe and punitive in nature, that are intended to be applied re-gardless of the gravity of behavior, mitigating circumstances, or situation con-text. Such policies appear to be widespread in America's schools, although the lack of a single definition of zero tolerance makes it difficult to estimate how prevalent such policies may be. (p. 852)

Such policies, while logical in nature, have the effect of increasing a stu-dent's likelihood of interacting with police and the criminal justice system in the future.

While one could certainly argue that there is a benefit to removing some students from the school (either temporarily or permanently), there is no educational value or rehabilitative nature to punitive punishments. Further, it harms students academically by removing them from a structured, education-al environment (which troubled students need more than most) and provides them time to interact with other people at home or in the community who may not have jobs or educational concerns.

Yes, schools have a duty to protect students who follow the rules and want to learn, but there needs to be a community effort to rehabilitate chil-dren who show signs of troubling behavior, lest it turn into criminal behavior in the future. When students are abandoned or exiled by institutions that have been charged with educating, informing, and supporting their growth, it sends a literal and symbolic message that the school has given up on them and they are irredeemable.

As the NAACP Legal Defense Fund (2008) explains,

> Studies have shown that a child who has been suspended is more likely to be retained in grade, to drop out, to commit a crime, and/or to end up incarcerated as an adult. Indeed, many schools are further expediting the flow of children out of the schools and into the criminal justice system by doling out a double dose of punishment and [referring them to law enforcement or juvenile course and prosecuted for behavior at school]. (p. 3)

Though it seems school districts and administrators may have their hands tied in addressing increasingly problematic behavior, the Children's Defense Fund (2007) published a report on the school-to-prison pipeline offering nine suggestions for schools to consider when evaluating their disciplinary processes. These suggestions are available in appendix C, with a link to the full report.

Severing Social Bonds

As noted in chapter 1, social bonds are relationships to people or institutions that students create as a level of control to not engage in delinquency. Because people feel attached and committed, they are less likely to commit crimes or do anything to jeopardize their relationships or disappoint those whom they trust and love. For many students, especially those who are already exhibiting problematic behavior, social bonds may, in fact, be the way to encourage them to change their ways.

By providing more support, promoting prosocial behavior, and approaching the issue through a more rehabilitative lens, school employees may create relationships rather than severing them through suspensions and expulsions. If these students are kept in school with a more preventative approach, they may be more inclined to feel supported.

Especially when students do not feel that discipline policies are distributed fairly, students see discipline used as a tool against all students, not simply ones who misbehave. As noted by the Chicago Consortium (Steinberg, Allensworth, & Johnson, 2011), "The heavy reliance on punitive disciplinary measures as a means of enforcing safety and order ends up making students feel less in control, less respected and cared for, and ultimately, less safe" (p. 35).

Contribution to Racial Disparities

In addition to the concern that the school-to-prison pipeline funnels children into the criminal justice system through harsh punishment, there is also the issue of the disparities between white students and students of color. As the NAACP Legal Defense Fund (2008) notes, "African Americans, especially young black males, have felt the brunt of the dramatic policy shift away from education and towards incarceration. . . . Studies show that African American students are far more likely than their white peers to be suspended, expelled, or arrested for the *same kind* of conduct at school" (p. 6). Whether due to an underlying belief that young black males are more aggressive, the achievement gap, implicit bias, poorly resourced schools, undertrained staff in prevention and conflict resolution, or parental influence on behavior and child-rearing, the disparities are clear.

Numerous studies have consistently found that African American students are overrepresented in nationwide suspension rates, and that it is not simply due to economic disadvantage. Combined with modern issues of standardized testing, this trend can be alarming. As the NAACP Legal Defense

Fund (2008) wrote, "Hallmarks of modern education reform . . . actually encourage schools to funnel out those students whom they believe are likely to drag down a school's test scores" (p. 5).

Other Unintended Consequences

Unfortunately, the problems do not simply involve the school-to-prison pipeline and overrepresentation of minorities. There are other important aspects to consider when thinking about punishment and school safety. Perhaps the most important is noting the crucial balance between safety and perceptions of fear. While physical security may be necessary, especially in an era of prominent mass shootings grabbing the headlines, the use of prominent, visible security measures may also have negative effects on student and faculty perceptions.

Many may understand the need for them, but in other schools and for many students, it may be a visual reminder that such measures are necessary. Take, for example, a moment to think about when you have taken a wrong turn into a neighborhood with which you were unfamiliar. If you saw multiple police officers around or bars on the windows (essentially, safety measures to protect you), you would likely feel as though you were in a bad part of town. The same may occur with schools. Similarly, if you remember the infamous line from *Lean on Me*, Joe Clark proclaimed, "And tear down those cages in the cafeteria! You treat them like animals, that's exactly how they'll behave."

In addition to the prisonization of schools and harsher punishments, schools that have notoriously strict policies and measures tend to get labeled as "bad" or "rough." While some students (and employees) wear that as a badge of honor, other students may find it difficult to fight back against the stigma that comes with it.

If negative labels on the community, schools, and individuals become strong enough, they almost become self-fulfilling prophecies that are easier to accept than to challenge. [2] Especially in cities that often make the dubious list of "the most dangerous cities in the country," those who live there may feel overlooked, stigmatized, or stereotyped by the actions of others.

Lastly, in communities that have already been damaged by mass incarceration, the school-to-prison pipeline perpetuates the problem. Even worse, it engages new generations of children with the criminal justice system, which is both costly and detrimental to society at large, given the financial and social costs of incarceration. Newer programs focused on restorative justice practices [3] have found success in schools (and in communities) in reducing recidivism rates and changing behaviors by creating specific rehabilitative and tailored punishments that aim to repair the harm that the student has done to the school and communities. In addressing crime and delinquency as damaging to a larger community, it may prevent future delinquency and stop the flow of the school-to-prison pipeline.

CONCLUSION

In sum, the effects of disorder and violence are important to consider when thinking about how to make schools safer. Thinking about the impact on teachers, students, and communities can be overwhelming. However, keeping an eye toward progress and positive change, schools can implement preventative and conflict resolution strategies that can reduce violent incidents. By focusing on small-scale changes, research-based policies, and tailored responses that are founded on theories and evidence, schools can begin a path toward safety and security that helps all students and minimizes the harm done by punitive policies.

NOTES

1. The original study was outlined in a paper presented in French at a conference in Italy: Janosz, M., Thiébaud, M., Bouthillier, C., & Brunet, L. (2004). Perception du climat scolaire et épuisement professionnel chez les enseignants [Perceived school climate and teacher burnout]. Paper presented at the XIII Congrès AIPTLF de psychologie du travail et des organisations, Bologna, Italy.

2. This idea is supported by the criminological theory of *labeling*. It asserts that behavior can be influenced by the notions used to describe them, as in a self-fulfilling prophecy. For more information, read Howard Becker's (1963) groundbreaking book *Outsiders*.

3. Evaluations of restorative justice practices in school have been overwhelmingly positive. For more information, read Anita Wadhwa's *Restorative justice in urban schools: Disrupting the school to prison pipeline* (New York: Routledge, 2016). It is a relatively quick read and offers a brief history of restorative justice in the United States, its application in schools, and the challenges it presents, while also offering qualitative insights.

Chapter Four

Slow Down the Violence

Peace is not the absence of conflict, but the presence of creative alternatives for responding to conflict.

—Dorothy Thompson

With theories, statistics, and strategies, it now becomes imperative that you think specifically about acts of violence and conflicts that you may encounter at work. Part of this exercise requires you to think about your own abilities, thought processes, and rationale so that you can create a plan, prepare for the situation, and understand your role and risk.

As an employee of the school, at the very least, it is important to examine your own strengths (and limitations) and trust your instincts. States require schools to practice fire drills and lockdown drills; similarly, individuals need to understand the best course of action and familiarize themselves with the process, especially in the absence of clear guidelines and expectations from administration.

School boards and administrators tend to avoid making clear-cut recommendations or policies for the role of employees in physical conflict. This is understandable, as a written policy proscribing a hands-off approach may result in liability in the event of a severe injury to a student, while encouraging employees to physically intervene may leave them responsible for injuries incurred to the adults. It is certainly a difficult situation, but in the absence of any policy, guidance, recommendations, or suggestions, there is much more room for variation in outcomes. Such variation could range from nonviolence to a quick suppression to a violent conflict.

This chapter outlines ways for you to think about situations, identify factors that affect your decisions, and help your school make well-considered decisions without formally introducing policy. It is imperative to note, though, that these are tips for developing skills. They are not simple tasks that one can learn and implement overnight, but rather come with practice and experience.

Also, I am not ignorant of the fact that school employees are tasked with many responsibilities and duties that require them to spread thin their time, effort, and attention. Through practice, however, and simple observations, these strategies may become instinctive rather than laborious tasks. And, if this book and schools can expedite the decision-making process using these tools and strategies, it may prevent or suppress violence.

BEFORE THE FIGHT: THE CALM BEFORE THE STORM?

Some school employees have a sixth sense about violence. They may not be able to explain their reasoning precisely, but they know when the students are on edge and recognize "a change in the air" before a fistfight breaks out. A teacher once described it as "a sizzling feeling . . . a pressure cooker when the students are on edge and everyone just feels anxious."

Another compared it to "walking down the street in New York City where everyone is guarded and anxious, but it's all condensed in the hallway of your workplace." Other employees claim that it correlates with weather, the holidays, or even a full moon.

Some teachers, administrators, and employees, however, do not notice the feeling. They may be mired in professional responsibilities or preoccupied with an exciting lesson they are planning. Others are not necessarily attuned to the social cues that students may offer, or they may be simply unable to recognize these cues. This is not intended to attribute blame, especially in light of the fact that these lessons are often overlooked in teacher education and preparation programs.

Obviously, this book cannot provide you with certain "Spidey senses" to know when violence will occur, but it can offer warning signs and strategies that you can utilize to prevent a conflict before it occurs. Steps to take before a conflict occurs are summarized in table 4.1.

The best teachers and school employees often seem superhuman (or are expected to be) in their abilities to multitask, divide their attention, and engage children in learning activities. They can provide individual instruction to a struggling child and simultaneously give the "teacher look" to another student who looks like he might be *considering* something disruptive. "A head on a swivel" is a profound understatement for many teachers.

Step 1: Know Your Students

First and foremost, the best teachers and school employees know their students, and they know them well. They know the average temperament for their students, their personalities, their friend groups, and their emotional

Table 4.1.   A Summary of the Steps

Step	Goal	Individual Level	School Level
Step 1	Know your students	*Know their personalities so that you can sense changes and problems.*	*Reward and praise teaching practices that build a teacher-student rapport.*
Step 2	Greet your students at the door	*Use a quick greeting to engage the students and gauge their attitudes before class.*	*Mandate that teachers stand at the doorway or in the hallways between classes.*
Step 3	Listen to their side conversations	*Listen when they talk about problems and conflicts that may escalate to violence.*	*Encourage teachers to move around the classroom during group exercises.*
Step 4	Get them to talk	*Ask questions that will lend information toward a peaceful resolution.*	*Provide training for de-escalation and talking strategies.*
Step 5	Utilize student personnel services and other resources	*Identify people, practices, and resources that may help in the event of a conflict.*	*Offer plans and procedures at the beginning of and throughout the year.*
Step 6	Know your role	*Decide if you should be an active or passive bystander.*	*Assert that during a conflict, employees must do something (either through active or passive intervention).*
Step 7	Plan your action	*Examine yourself and your own limitations to decide on a course of action in a variety of scenarios.*	*Plan accordingly when scheduling, especially in large areas like bus loading and the cafeteria.*

triggers. Even more, they know how each student speaks and behaves, so they recognize a change in a student's tone of voice or if he is no longer speaking to a friend.

School employees often learn about their students through a variety of different strategies. Many classroom teachers assign their students projects or tasks that reveal a personal element; others ask students specific questions to learn more about them. English teachers, for example, can provide writing prompts for their students to write about their families, a problem that has been bothering them, or issues they see in schools. Other teachers can take a moment or two of class time to talk to their students and ask how their day is going or find out what has been happening among students. The most engaging teachers can mix the two and incorporate the students' own experiences and personalities into learning.

Active strategies can be extremely useful in getting to your students, but the best way to get to know your students is to simply observe them. Watch them in the classroom, and examine how they interact with their peers. Know who their friends are in class, and gauge their temperaments. Be perceptive to how they perceive themselves, their academic and social abilities, and their surroundings. By being attentive to these nuances in addition to their academic achievements and abilities, you may also improve their learning experiences by identifying ways to help them in the classroom.

This step also helps to create a better rapport with your students, to engage them further and encourage them to create social bonds with the school and individuals at the school, and alert you to other issues like family problems, poverty, homelessness, suicidal behavior, mental illness, or delinquency.

Step 2: Greet Your Students at the Door

Schools often require or urge teachers to stand in the hallways outside of their classrooms in between classes. Typically, this is to provide guardianship in the hallways that are dense with students. This can, however, also function as a way to gauge your students' emotional status for the day. Going back to the ABCs of psychology, this gives you the very clear opportunity to observe each student's unique affect and behavior as he or she enters the room. As noted in step 1, this becomes more important and useful as you grow your relationship with students so that you can notice changes or deviations from their normal behavior.

Other teachers prefer to do this at the start of class as a sort of checking in with the students. This can be a quick index card activity or a conversation as you take attendance or while you wait for students to prepare for class. One teacher uses a strategy every Friday in which she asks each class to name "one good thing" and "one bad thing" that happened each week. It is simple enough for the students and creates a strong relationship with them, but it also provides her with insight about them to close out the week.

When students enter the room and have a noticeable behavioral change or problem, this is an ideal time to move them away from their peers and get them to talk (step 4). This is not as confrontational as a one-on-one interaction in front of the class, but it also prevents the student's mood or behavior from affecting the entire class and their own learning.

If students are upset or distracted, they will likely learn little or nothing during the class (and potentially for the rest of the day). However, if the teacher can address the problem and either solve it immediately or connect them to someone who can help, it has the potential to save the rest of the day and avoid any conflict that may occur later.

Some teachers may lament that they have limited time with students to achieve the day's goals, prepare for state tests, and administer benchmark exams. It is undoubtedly difficult to address student problems in the context of a larger school environment that has important deadlines and objectives. However, a student missing one class to resolve a conflict may prevent the student from missing multiple days of class due to a suspension for fighting. Moreover, if the student is more focused after effectively addressing the issue, they are more apt to learn, perform better, and retain the information presented to them.

Step 3: Listen to Their Side Conversations

In a perfect world, when students engage in group work or collaborative experiences, they are so engrossed in the topic that they excitedly discuss your guiding questions or scribble their thoughts furiously on the papers that you have provided for them. What most teachers know is that we do not live in a perfect world, and that students may get distracted by conversations about everything except the topic at hand.

As all administrators and education professors assert, group work requires the teacher to move from group to group, assisting students and keeping them focused on the task at hand. They should, however, be alert to other conversations that are happening simultaneously.

Rather than simply chastising students for talking about other students who are having a problem, teachers can take a moment to ask the students who they are talking about and what the issue is. Listening for keywords like obscenities, "problem," or "fight" may train teachers to zero in and filter through other conversations about sports or pop culture.

Veteran teachers who read this are likely to find this to be old hat, as they have learned this through experience and years of practice. The purpose, again, with these steps is to provide all employees, new and seasoned, with tools to fast-forward them through the learning curve and encourage them to practice their skills every day to prevent school violence.

Further, this gives administrators an observable opportunity to provide positive feedback to encourage and inform teachers that they are on the right track in learning to sense conflicts and prevent violence.

Step 4: Get Them to Talk

An educator once explained his way of addressing questionable or undesirable behavior. He said that he would simply ask the student, "Is everything okay?" It is quick, simple, and nonconfrontational, but almost every time, it elicited the same response: "Yep." The question—and the minimalist re-sponse—does not allow for the educator to explain his concern and address the behavior, nor does it require the student to say more. Parents of teenagers have undoubtedly asked, "How was your day today?" and received the oblig-atory "Fine" before their child goes to her room and shuts the door.

If you notice a student who is markedly depressed, upset, angry, or for-lorn, the first step is to ask her to step aside and talk to her. By asking the types of questions that require longer responses, school employees may draw explanations from the students so that they can address the problem or direct her to someone else who can (see table 4.2 for tips).

Most importantly, though, yes or no questions are mostly useless in this situation. If an adolescent who is reluctant to speak about a problem is offered a yes or no question, a yes or no response is likely all she will offer, unless she is familiar or comfortable with the teacher. Remember, too, the personal fable. For a teenager, this problem is the only time that this problem has affected anyone, and you, the teacher, would never understand the tragic agony of her dilemma.

"What's wrong?" is often a good place to start, although the obvious, avoidant response is "nothing." This is the time to acknowledge your obser-vations and let her know that you do, in fact, know that there is a problem. "You're acting much different than usual today. You're usually so happy, and I'm concerned. What can I do to make this better?" Not only are you offering your concern and attention to the student, but you are also offering her the opportunity for help. If she still refuses, you may consider offering suggestions like letting her work in the library for the class period, going to

Table 4.2.   Tips for Talking

Do	*Don't*
• Speak calmly and slowly • Ask questions that delve into the problem • Observe body language (e.g., flared nostrils, clenched fists, jittery behavior) • Use your body position to create privacy for the student • Express your level of concern • Cite the reasons for your concern • Offer possible solutions and courses of action • Ask the student to count backwards and then explain • Seek out assistance from another staff member	• Immediately chastise the student for profanity or provocative language • Interrogate the student in a confrontational way • Raise your voice at the student • Attempt to touch the student if he exhibits clear signs of anger • Ask yes or no questions that allow the student to disengage

speak to a counselor, or talking after class if she does not seem to be doing any better.

Reticent students present their own challenges and require the adult to ask the magic question that will get them to talk. There are other students, though, whose behavior will leave you with little doubt that something is wrong. A student once entered the classroom shouting at her friends, "If that [expletive] thinks she can look at my boyfriend, she better think again before I punch her in the [expletive] mouth." Clearly, there is a problem here, and the teacher must address this issue (not simply the profanity) lest it become a bigger issue later in the day.

Again, separating this student from the other students and asking questions may lead to more information that would allow administrators to intervene in the problem. By simply asking, "Why are you yelling?" this student will likely tell you who exactly she plans on punching, who her boyfriend is, and perhaps other important details of the issue.

In some cases, students may be illogical or irrational in their explanations or simply be too upset to talk. A teacher once attempted to ask a student what was wrong, and he stood there, breathing heavily with his nostrils flaring, as he was too angry to form sentences. In this moment, it helps to use the counseling strategy and advise the student to "count backward from 10 and then tell me what's wrong." Sometimes, even a bit of humor in the situation helps. "On second thought, you look really mad. Maybe count backward from 1,000."

If the student does not crack a smile or even understand what you said, the student may be so engrossed in his anger or sadness that he is unable to hear you speak. In these moments, a teacher should request assistance from a counselor or ask another teacher to move him to a quiet area where he can calm down, regroup, and then address the issue with an adult.

Another important piece of this step is moving the location where the conversation is taking place and using subtle physical steps to calm the student. When addressing the student, it is best to separate him from peers, as he is less likely to speak to you openly and honestly if there is an audience. By speaking to him in the hallway, out of the line of vision of the other students, he feels as though the interaction is more intimate. If he can still see his peers, he may be able to physically see the person with whom he has a problem (which may aggravate him further), or the "imaginary audience" of his peers might be, in fact, a real audience. Simply repositioning your own body, or moving so that he must turn to face you, creates a more comfortable environment. You can also verbally initiate a move by saying, "Why don't you come over here and tell me what's wrong?"

Adolescents and teenagers, especially those in the throes of their emotions, lack the ability to truly think clearly, and educators must remember this in their interactions. In one situation, a principal and counselor were in an office speaking with two students who had a verbal conflict with another group of students. The two students were relatively calm in the moment in their explanations until two boys from the other group passed in the hallway with a security officer. The students in the office immediately jumped from their chairs and began yelling, which then caught the attention of the passing students who, in turn, began to yell and make threats.

The principal and counselor immediately jumped up to calm the situation, while the security officer in the hallway attempted to calm the boys for which he was responsible. During the short melee, the principal's secretary pulled down the shade over the door's window, and that essentially ended the commotion. Without the ability to see their opponent, the boys could return to a relatively rational state and think clearly. This story provides a strong example of the ways in which physical location, line of vision, and quick thinking can affect the outcome of an event.

Step 5: Utilize Student Personnel Services and Other Resources

In these scenarios, it becomes important to know what you can do and when it is time to seek out others for help. You must be aware of where students can find further support that you may not be able to offer. You may want to consider asking a nearby or passing teacher on a prep period to escort the student to a counselor or a principal. Conversely, someone from the office could come to the class to walk the student.

The student could certainly walk to another office alone, but he could also choose to go somewhere else (thus landing him in more trouble later), or even attempt to seek out the person who wronged him. This is a judgment call on the part of the teacher or school employee, but it is always best to err on the side of caution and use the information that you have at hand to make your decision.

For teachers who are new, the school should provide clearly stated procedures for addressing conflicts or students who are experiencing stress. Similarly, school administrators would be wise to remind all teachers and school personnel of these expectations and procedures at the yearly opening faculty meeting. This may include suggestions like this list, but should also instruct employees who to call, what information they should provide, and alternative courses of action if their first contact person is unavailable. Additionally, all school employees would benefit from an easy-to-read list of contact information that is readily available.

For schools that require employees to wear identification badges, the back may be used for a sticker with security, administrator, and counselor extensions. If identification stickers are unreasonable, provide teachers with a large-print, laminated page with the information to tape on the wall or near the door. This quick access reference sheet is a simple, yet effective way to request immediate help or assistance in a moment when a teacher may need it most. Teachers and employees may choose to do this on their own if the schools will not consider this as an option, but a schoolwide plan to provide clear communication options for everyone is clearly the ideal approach.

When phone calls are impossible due to a classroom full of students, email can be a useful tool. A high school teacher once smelled marijuana in her classroom, and it seemed that making a phone call to report it would cause an uproar. Instead, she opted to send an email to any administrator she could think of who may have been nearby or available. She quickly wrote, "There is a distinct odor of marijuana in my room, and I didn't want to call for fear that the students may react negatively or attempt to flush the drugs. Please come to my room immediately." Of the seven administrators she emailed, three saw her email and came to her room within minutes. (The others were addressing other student issues or were on their lunch break.) The issue was resolved before the students realized that the teacher had even noticed.

In another situation, a teacher noticed that a student still had his hood up in class. When she asked him to remove it, he refused not by speaking, but simply shaking his head. She knelt next to him to find out what the problem was and noticed several cuts on his face. She asked him to step outside into the hallway to talk, but he would not speak and did not make any motion to move. The other students were working in paired assignments, so they did not necessarily notice what was happening. The teacher, realizing the urgency of the situation, decided not to call and request help (for fear of upsetting the student), but to send an email to all the school counselors requesting assistance. They arrived and the student went with them without incident, and the other students barely noticed.

For individual employees who have not received this training or information, it may be most helpful for them to contact administrators and counselors directly and ask what the best practice would be when they need assistance. This sends a message that you are proactive and prepared to address issues with the help of the school community. The administrators may offer the best school-specific responses or creative insight that you may not have otherwise considered.

Lastly, given the structure of many schools, the same school employees are often in close proximity all day. It may be helpful in the early days of the school year to familiarize yourself with those who work near you. Know when nearby teachers or employees have free periods so that you are aware of those who may be able to help if you need to address a problem.

Step 6: Know Your Role

In conflicts, particularly ones that include physical violence, there are multiple roles that students, teachers, and school employees can play. These roles are not always clearly identifiable, especially in the chaos of the moment, but they generally include aggressors, victims, and third parties (figure 4.1). Without knowing the facts of the situation or clearly observing the buildup, it may be impossible to identify who exactly is the aggressor and who is the victim if a fight appears evenly matched or is happening quickly. Regardless of the title, there is violence occurring, and someone needs to stop it.

Third parties may be the key. Cooney (1998) noted that a third party can play one of three roles: inciter, active bystander, and passive bystander.

Inciters often encourage the fight. They are not actively engaged in the fight by committing violence, but their participation allows it to continue. They may gather around, cheer on those involved, or record the incident on their phones. Their enthusiasm about the fight perpetuates the excitement and the fervor. These third-party inciters contribute to what Collins (2013) dubbed "the tunnel of violence." As he explains,

> [The crowd provides] a necessary backdrop to the small clusters of violent [people], by cheering or otherwise just making noise; they provide the emotional support that enables the violent elite to keep up their emotional energy. The crowd creates an emotional attention space, the center of which is occupied by the violent [students]. They are the center of attention, and know that they are. (p. 143)

For schools, one challenge of physical violence is the enthusiasm of the student observers. College students, when asked about fights in their high school, said that they always ran to watch because, "It was fun!" or "It was like watching UFC in person!" Unfortunately, congregation around the fight also creates a problem for active third parties.

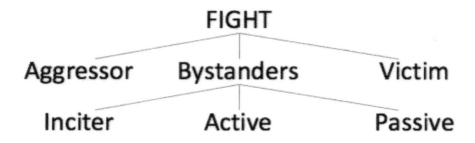

Figure 4.1.   Roles in a conflict.

Active third parties are those who engage in the conflict to end it. Such observers are typically school employees, such as school resource officers or willing school staff who will intervene. When they come upon the violent interaction, they may have difficulty gaining access to the fight due to the crowd of inciters. At one school, during fights the student inciters gathered around the fighters and linked arms to prevent school faculty from intervening.

Active third parties are not always school employees. Students can serve as active third parties by attempting to move the fighting students out of the fight. One teacher recalled a situation in which two students were violently attacking each other in her classroom in between class periods, and a third student entered the room to help the teacher restrain the students and end the fight.

Additionally, there are third parties who may engage in the fight in order to continue it or support the aggressors or the victims. Their decision to intervene may be affected by their relationships (and relational proximity) to those fighting and the expected gain from their participation. Their engagement in the fight accelerates and amplifies the conflict, and creates a larger problem for those responsible for ending it.

Passive third-party witnesses are those who do not engage directly in the fight but can still have some impact on the outcome or assist active third parties. School employees, as passive third-party actors, can serve as witnesses and document the details, call for help, assist security and other employees, or move students and maintain order. Students can also serve in some of these roles, but such behavior is typically assigned to the adults. Third-party adults also have the option of doing nothing, but this may be problematic for reasons discussed later.

Step 7: Plan Your Action

Looking at violence, conflicts, and schools using a prevention mind-set requires a breakdown of the components and factors that affect outcomes. The outcome (or dependent variable) in this scenario, presented in figure 4.2, is your own decision to intervene when confronted with violence. Three major factors that may affect your behavior and decisions are: self (meaning you, the reader), the situation, and the students. By examining each of these factors and the components that affect your perceptions, it may be helpful in predicting your personal behavior, your limitations, and your decision-making.

Students

In a casual conversation, a high school teacher was asked what factors affect his decision to help in a fight. As a joke, he responded, "It depends how

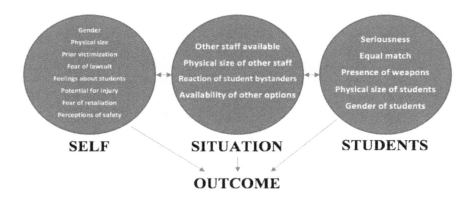

SELF   SITUATION   STUDENTS

OUTCOME

Figure 4.2.   Factors in employee decision making.

much I like the kid getting beat up." While this was a rather uncouth joke, it highlights the ways that some teachers and school employees may think about fights.

If you saw two students engaged in a fight, what would you notice first? The seriousness and severity of the fight? The size and gender of the students? Whether you realize it or not, these are variables that will likely affect your decision to intervene. Perhaps it is not necessarily a fair fight, and one student is being badly beaten by the other. Maybe a female student is being assaulted by a male student. Would these make you more likely to intervene? If it were two large male students who were known to be excessively violent, would you choose to avoid the fight instead? What if the participants were two female students? Weapon carrying is relatively rare among students, but if you were to see a weapon, would you be more or less likely to attempt to stop the fight?

While these are all factors to consider and acknowledge in your own decision-making process, they are not necessarily ones that can be altered. In fact, these are the variables that will change from incident to incident and serve as the impetus for your action. While certain school policies and practices may limit student-related factors (like metal detectors that prevent weapon carrying), these are, for the most part, variables that you should consider in your own planning. Yet, these are not part of prevention or intervention options for future efforts to predict outcomes.

Situation

While the students present unique combinations of factors, so does the situation itself. These factors are often highly variable and easily adjustable. For example, student fights often occur in areas where the student-to-teacher ratio is high. Common areas such as the bus loading zones, the cafeteria, and hallways lend themselves to conflict simply due to the density of students and the lack of capable guardianship. A young teacher who had lunch duty for a semester noted that she was in a cafeteria with 300 students and 4 other teachers. Of her colleagues, two were more than 60 years old, one was especially diminutive and had already expressed her lack of interest in policing the students, and the fourth was a bodybuilder. She realized that in the event of a melee, there would likely be only two teachers to address the conflict among 300 students.

In this scenario, the availability of other staff would likely affect this teacher's decision making, especially in combination with the student factors listed previously. She may be somewhat hesitant to intervene, but may be compelled otherwise if she saw that the other employees were unwilling to help. Conversely, she may be even less likely to intervene given the lack of support that she would receive.

This type of problem lends itself nicely to a few simple, yet effective school practices that administrators can implement using logic and common sense. First, larger schools can focus on the teacher-to-student ratio in common areas, with an ideal goal being 1 teacher for every 40 students. While still high, such a ratio would have provided at least three additional teachers in the scenario listed above.

Second, school administrators can plan accordingly when assigning teachers to such common areas. Though creating schedules can often be something like an infuriating game of Sudoku, a bit of practicality can go a long way. Consider the age, gender, physical build, attitude, and athleticism of the teachers when assigning and scheduling them to monitor common areas that are dense with students. Try to pair older or fragile teachers with other teachers who may be able to provide more support. Recall times that teachers have avoided or intervened in previous conflicts, and use that knowledge to distribute abilities evenly. Administrators may find it helpful to rank each available teacher using a scale of 1 (not likely to intervene) to 3 (very likely to intervene), and aim for an average score of 2 for all those scheduled in the same area.

Next, schools can create alternative actions for teachers who choose not to physically intervene in the event of a fight. A cost-effective solution such as walkie-talkies can provide a reasonable strategy for calling for assistance. Teachers and employees can also be encouraged to immediately leave to get help from security or administrators. This may be helpful as an option for those who strongly assert or know that they will not engage in any type of physical contact with students. Administrators may also offer them the option of moving students away from the conflict or creating a path through the crowd for others to successfully intervene.

Lastly, the students as bystanders are likely to play an active role in the violence by creating a commotion that encourages the students fighting or by impeding the path to end the conflict. This is profoundly difficult for schools to address, as the school employees are nearly always outnumbered by students. However, if there are more employees present as noted previously, it may make the situation more manageable and end the commotion more quickly.

Self

The factor that is easiest to address at this very moment is you. If you take the time to examine your own role in a situation, you will be better suited to make an effective, split-second decision. Think about your own physical presentation, including your gender, age, physicality, and athleticism. Consider any injuries or disabilities that may limit your potential to intervene in or end violence. These are relatively stable factors that will affect your decision making and help you to sort out your feelings and perceptions about violence.

Next, consider your own fears and how they affect your thinking about the situation. Have you been victimized or injured at work before? In a 2013 study, 80 percent of more than 3,000 teachers surveyed reported at least one victimization in the current or past year. This included incidents of harassment, property offenses, and physical attacks (Espelage et al., 2013). Such incidents of victimization against teachers can affect the ways that they think about violence and increase perceptions of fear. How does this compare to your ideas about violence and safety in your school, and how will it affect your interventions?

One important aspect to consider is your fear about intervention. What scares you most about intervening in a fight: a lawsuit, injury, or retaliation from the students? Is it all three? You need to think about possibilities, the likelihood of each, and how willing you are to risk them compared to the possibility of severe student injury in a fight. There is, without a doubt, an increased likelihood of harm to you if you decide to engage in a physical conflict between students. This cannot be ignored, and you need to consider it as you plan your course of action.

In order to prepare yourself and know what your role will be in the face of violence, examine your abilities and consider the consequences and risks. Think about all possible scenarios, as you did when you examined the student factors earlier. Consider your own hard boundaries and situations in which you refuse to engage. What will you do if you are not an active participant in the physical conflict?

PREDICTING OUTCOMES

The purpose of the exercise is to encourage you to think about conflicts in an organized, logical way as a form of preparation and reflection. It is helpful to understand the ways in which these individual, situational, and student-centered factors come together to help you decide if you should intervene in or avoid a conflict. Essentially, individuals and schools need to consider these variables to predict outcomes and alter variables to create the greatest likelihood for a nonviolent or quickly suppressed incident.

There are few studies that examine teacher and school employee decision making. Even more importantly, there are no known studies to date about factors that result in nonviolence. In criminology and education studies, nonviolence is rarely an outcome that is studied, as it is hard to conceptualize and operationalize a variable that does not exist. This makes prediction incredibly difficult.

There are statistical and mathematical ways to predict and influence outcomes. In addition to criminology, there are many disciplines that rely on regression modeling to make predictions. Other social sciences, business, and the hard sciences use statistics and data to explain causal relationships between variables. In doing so, the goal is to identify the factors that affect outcomes. In a real-world application, regression models can be incredibly useful to study school conflicts.

Note that some of these factors discussed, such as gender and physical size of both employees and students, are variables that cannot be changed. From an intervention and prevention perspective, the goal is to adjust other variables that can, in fact, be modified to affect the outcome. Recalling that students are impulsive and hasty to engage in conflict, it becomes more useful for the school to focus on individual actions and the elements of the situation that can be controlled.

Clearly, there are constant efforts to assist students, provide academic and personal support, and engage students in positive school activities. In planning for addressing conflicts, the goal is to control as many variables as possible. Students, in this exercise, are the least likely to be controlled or changed, so the individual employees and situations should be the focus of the interventions. If there are a multitude of variables over which school administrators and employees have little control, there is little possibility of controlling the outcome, which, in the worst-case scenario, is violence and harm to students or teachers.

Chapter Five

Program Design and Implementation

For tomorrow belongs to the people who prepare for it today.
—African proverb

Thus far, this book has provided some theoretical frameworks for understanding violence, examined the research on the frequency and effects of school violence, evaluated policies and practices that work, and suggested individual and schoolwide policies that may offer effective outcomes in the face of conflicts. While the previous chapters have focused on individual approaches and planning, this chapter provides a detailed way for schools to create programs or policies that can prevent or reduce violence. This chapter first examines the various types of interventions and programs, and then provides a step-by-step outline for those who wish to develop school-specific programs to address the issues that their educators and students face.

INTERVENTIONS

In the moment of a conflict, the term "intervention" is used to describe the actions of those nearby who may intercede to mediate the problem. Teachers, resource officers, and other school staff can intervene to end a fight. However, in the larger context, an intervention can also be an effective program or policy that schools implement to reduce school violence issues and effect change. They can be large-scale in nature, such as a schoolwide plan to create respectful behavior and reward compliance and nonviolence, or they can be focused and targeted at a small, specific group of students who are most at risk.

The feasibility and success of each of these types of interventions depends on the nature of the problem, the size of the school, and the resources that are available to properly implement, monitor, and evaluate the program. Many schools already have procedures, policies, and mechanisms in place to address problematic behavior, and these types of interventions are useful in tackling issues at hand. There are ways, however, to streamline these processes and ensure that they are effective in creating long-term change and a safer environment for all students and school employees.

A Framework for Safe and Successful Schools, a joint statement from educator organizations and mental health supporters, offered best practices to support school safety.[1] Among these was the recommendation to "implement multitiered systems of support (MTSS) that encompass prevention, wellness promotion, and interventions that increase with intensity based on student need, and that promote close school-community collaboration" (Cowan, Vaillancourt, Rossen, & Pollitt, 2013, p. 1). This is the goal for all schools, but again, it is reasonable to acknowledge that such comprehensive planning is often difficult in the context of the competing demands of the school. As such, it becomes important to prioritize the issues and then identify the beginnings of an intervention that may be best suited for a specific school. The various levels of interventions are important to understand when moving forward, as they differ in their target populations, goals, and approaches.

Universal Interventions

Universal interventions address the entire school and often aim to change the school climate. As Gagnon and Leone (2001) note,

> Schoolwide or universal interventions attempt to create school and classroom climates for all children that promote social and academic growth and a sense of community. These interventions endeavor to create a culture within the school in which respect for the individual, predictability, and the perception of fair play shape the behavior of teachers, students, and administrators. (p. 104)

In this sense, the approach aims to teach and model appropriate behavior for students, address all teachers and employees using schoolwide initiatives, or offer consistent responses for behavioral expectations and misconduct.

The National Center on Education, Disability and Juvenile Justice offers a number of best practices and promising practices for universal interventions including, but not limited to, developing a link between school and community, active supervision, error correction, and praise for desired behavior.[2] The Center also provides research that supports these practices as stand-alone measures as well as part of implementation in a larger program.

There are organizations and companies that provide these types of universal interventions and clearly outline how the programs should be implemented in schools. One of the most well-known is termed Positive Behavior Interventions & Supports (PBIS). Swain-Bradway, Johnson, Bradshaw, and

McIntosh (2017) estimated that cost to the school for a schoolwide PBIS program is $12,500 for training and staffing. The website describes the program's underlying theme as "teaching behavioral expectations in the same manner as any core curriculum subject" (PBIS, n.d., para. 1).[3]

The model also utilizes MTSS and focuses on universal interventions as tools for all students, with increasing targets and levels of intervention (referred to as "tiers"). The program cites significant empirical evidence that the methods and approaches are effective in improving perceptions of school safety and organizational health in schools that implement the practices. While the initial focus is on universal interventions, the program offers targeted and intensive interventions (or secondary and tertiary tiers, respectively) to address increasingly concerning academic or behavioral issues.

The Resolving Conflict Creatively Program (RCCP) is another well-known program that utilizes the universal intervention to address issues of school safety and conflicts. Designed for elementary and middle school students, it provides a curriculum designed to teach all students to communicate effectively, manage anger, mediate conflicts, and cooperate with their peers (Aber, Pedersen, Brown, Jones, & Gershoff, 2003). The foundation of the program asserts that aggression and violence is learned (in the same vein as Akers' social learning theory) and can therefore be reduced by using educational approaches.

RCCP lists the objectives of the program: "1. Reduce violence and violence-related behavior. 2. Promote caring and cooperative behavior. 3. Teach students life skills in conflict resolution and intercultural understanding. 4. Promote a positive climate for learning in the classroom and school" (Aber et al., 2003, p. 4). An in-depth program evaluation found that RCCP "can significantly reduce the rate in which [aggression and actual levels of aggressive behavior] increase," particularly during middle childhood (p. 6). This universal intervention approach aims to teach all students using the program curriculum. Evaluations have shown that the program leads to reduced aggression and violence in schools in which the program is implemented.

Newer iterations of the program include the 4Rs Program (Reading, Writing, Respect & Resolution) and Restore360. As described by researchers who evaluated the programs, "The 4Rs Program is a school-based intervention in literacy development, conflict resolution, and intergroup understanding that trains and supports all teachers in kindergarten through fifth grade in how to integrate the teaching of social and emotional skills into the language arts curriculum" (LaRusso & Aber, 2010, p. 156). Using an experimental design, an evaluation of the program found that children who participated in the program had fewer symptoms of depression, fewer symptoms of hyperactivity and attention problems, and lower levels of teacher-reported aggression (Jones, Brown, Hoglund, & Aber, 2010).

Such promising programs offer an overview of how effective universal interventions approach the issues of violence reduction and prevention. Aimed to address all students and improve the school culture, the effects may be far-reaching and improve conditions for teachers, employees, and students.

Targeted (Secondary) Interventions

Targeted interventions focus on specific groups of students through early identification and detection when students do not respond to universal interventions. Often referred to as Response to Intervention (RTI), targeted and intensive (or secondary and tertiary, respectively) interventions aim to provide preventative support before a student fails academically or behaviorally.

The National Center on Education, Disability and Juvenile Justice recommends implementing a team approach (an emerging practice) to manage these types of interventions, as the task may be too large in scope for one individual staff member. The team addresses academic, social, and psychological needs and meets frequently to monitor progress, find and implement resources, and most importantly, ensure that students are engaged in learning. By identifying students who need additional support to succeed behaviorally and modify potentially violent behavior, the school can provide the tailored, rehabilitative resources to address problems before they occur. It also notes reconnecting youth and providing and requesting family support as best practices.

Intensive (Tertiary) Interventions

Finally, students for whom targeted interventions are unsuccessful can benefit from the final tier involving intensive interventions. Like secondary or targeted interventions, these focus on specific students, but are designed specifically for students who continue with disruptive or negative behaviors even after targeted interventions have been implemented. At this point, it becomes necessary for the school to provide rigorous strategies in order to save the child.

While some may be frustrated by this point, given the short- and long-term consequences of punitive measures like suspension or expulsion, the school must consider every possible option to modify the child's behavior and find what works. Using evidence-based, data-driven interventions allows for a small percentage of students to receive the amount of attention and services that they need to be successful.

The National Center on Intensive Intervention offers studies of behavioral interventions and rates the quality of the study, provides the results, and offers program information to educators. The website[4] also provides behavioral progress charts for downloading, and it offers multiple scales for myriad problems including disruptive behaviors, conduct issues, social withdrawal, and others. Using empirically based programs, monitoring progress, adapting, and remonitoring allows for the most scientific, clear ways to address specific student needs.

ADDRESSING THE PROBLEMS: GOING AT IT ALONE?

While nationally recognized programs may offer curricula, trainings, support, and evaluation opportunities, school districts may be hesitant to buy in for any number of reasons. First, while these programs typically have a relatively low per student cost, schools may be unwilling or unable to devote limited funds to purchase all the necessary components.

Second, school administrators may feel that a universal intervention may not be optimal for their student population. They may also believe that their problems are far beyond the scope of a "quick fix" or a "cookie-cutter approach." Finally, schools are often hesitant to open their doors to outsiders who may be quick to judge or evaluate their current practices.

If, for whatever reason, a school is unwilling to participate or purchase pre-existing programs, administrators and employees can choose to create a program of their own that is tailored to the problems that they experience. This is certainly a valuable and important option, as those who work in the schools understand the problems best and are well-positioned to implement positive change.

The remainder of this chapter provides a nine-step method for schools to create their own programs and policies (see table 5.1). This does, however, require that motivated, informed members of the school community come together to tackle a problem and address it using a methodological, scientific approach.

CONVENE A SCHOOL SAFETY COMMITTEE

It is important for those reading this chapter to realize that this journey is not one to be traveled alone. Program and policy development and evaluation requires an almost frightening amount of work. Specifically, it demands collaboration, creativity, and discipline. The process relies on the exchange of ideas, varying levels of knowledge and expertise, and shared responsibility.

A school safety committee should be comprised of members (and representatives) of the school community who have the common goal of making the environment safer and more productive. Depending on the size of the school and the faculty, the committee should have between five and ten

Table 5.1.   Steps for Program/Policy Development and Implementation

Step 1	Identify the problem	*Ask the committee to focus on a specific problem*
Step 2	Examine scope and frequency	*Use data to identify the scope of the problem*
Step 3	Set goals and objectives	*Create measurable outcomes*
Step 4	Choose a theory	*Identify a framework for understanding the problem*
Step 5	Create an impact model	*Link the theory, the problem, and the solution*
Step 6	Plan	*Create a plan with deadlines and actionable items*
Step 7	Monitor	*Ensure that the program is implemented as planned*
Step 8	Evaluate outcomes	*Use data to decide if goals were met*
Step 9	Reassess and review	*Examine ways to improve and continue the program*

members that may include teachers, administrators, parents, school board members, students, security officers, counselors and social workers, and other school employees. Groups who are not represented or included in the core committee may be added as ad hoc members and consulted in the early stages of the planning (especially in the problem identification and data collection stages).

The group should have a set schedule for meetings throughout the year (see appendix D) and, in an ideal world, these meetings would occur after school, with members receiving a stipend for the additional hours and work that are required for effective and meaningful program or policy creation. In reality this may not be possible, but recurring, planned meetings and an understanding of shared responsibilities (including the ad hoc members) must be set from the start.

As with any collaborative project, especially in schools, personalities and intentions play an important role. Schools are often filled with "type A" employees who are idealistic, positive, and optimistic. These are the teachers, administrators, and staff members who always search for new ways to keep students engaged or tackle a problem, and these are likely to be the people who will leap at the chance to join a committee working to address school violence issues.

While a committee of optimists is a joy to imagine, their rose-colored glasses may lead them to overlook roadblocks, complications, or impediments. It is important, when selecting members to join, that you have at least one "yeah, but" person. "Yeah, but" people are still committed to solving problems and still mostly believe that there is a solution, but they often stop to point out ways that proposed solutions may not work. Optimists in schools tend to get frustrated when working with "yeah, but" people, but they are in fact helpful in keeping optimists and idealists grounded and in focusing on unintended consequences and worst-case scenarios.

The committee should indeed be comprised of a broad range of school roles, and there should be a focus on incorporating a heterogeneous mixture of personalities, approaches, and ideals. Members should all be hopeful and ready to address the problem, but their differences may lead them to create a program or policy that is well-balanced and creative.

As an added note, it may be useful to include someone who is comfortable with math and/or statistics in order to have a member who can analyze data and make use of the available information.

Step 1: Identify the Problem

A school may decide to convene a committee in order to address the issue of school violence, but it becomes necessary to identify the specific problem and define it in a clear, concise way that everyone on the committee agrees with and understands. School violence is a broad term. It could reflect issues like bullying, threatening, weapon carrying, gang issues, fighting, and more. If the school attempts to "fix everything," more often than not it will be addressing nothing.

Instead, the committee must decide on one problem that is clearly defined and outlined, and then commit to it. The problem can be discussed with parents, teachers, students, community members, school board members, administrators, and other school employees. These discussions can occur informally or through more formal measures such as focus groups, interviews, or surveys. The focus should always be student centered, and the question is, "What is the most pressing issue of violence that students face?" This should be in the context of learning and achievement, of course, so the problem should be one that affects teaching, learning, and perceptions of safety and fear at school.

As an example, in discussions the committee may be torn between fistfights and profanity as the two most pressing issues. Both can significantly disrupt the learning process, and the two issues result in frequent suspensions and missed class time for the students who engage in this behavior. The committee decides that "fistfights" are defined as "physical conflict between two or more students that includes punching and hitting." "Profanity" is "obscene language used by students directed at other students, employees, or teachers."

In order to decide which issue the committee should address, the 10 members must ask 20 people about which issue is more important, widespread, and pressing. They may ask people in the school community, record the responses, and email their findings to the group. At the next meeting, the group will discuss the findings, and then will vote on which issue to address. From there, the committee will decide how to gather data about the scope and frequency of the problem.

Step 2: Examine Scope and Frequency

At the following meeting, the committee needs to focus on this one specific problem. Members must decide which questions to ask, and what data are necessary to answer them. The best questions ask whom the problem affects, where and how often the problem occurs, why the problem is important (in terms of short- and long-term effects), what elements of current policies to address the problem are ineffective, and in which contexts the problem occurs. The purpose of this second meeting is to outline the data that will be collected before the next meeting and identify ways to outline the scope, frequency, and history of the problem.

Such an investigation will examine reasons why the problem is a pressing issue that the school faces. It will explain the scope of the problem, the ways in which it impedes learning and affects students and staff, and the history of the issue. The size of the committee will ultimately determine the amount and quality of the data to be gathered, but examples of information include formal surveys, interviews with relevant members of the school community, a review of the disciplinary reports, and examination of facilities and grounds (when relevant).

Whatever measures the committee chooses to use should answer the relevant questions (provided in appendix E) and serve to provide a broad and nuanced understanding of the problem. It may be difficult for school employees and administrators to acknowledge the school's shortcomings (or their own) in addressing the issue, but an honest and thoughtful evaluation of the problem will provide the best foundation for program or policy design and implementation.

In addition to gathering information about the frequency of occurrences, it is also important to note changes over time. Identify peaks and decreases in events and, as a committee, discuss potential reasons for the changes. Members will present the information that they find in the third meeting, and then use the remainder of the time to set goals and objectives.

Step 3: Set Goals and Objectives

At the third meeting, once the members have all presented the information about the scope, frequency, and history of the problem, the committee will decide what the overall goal will be. The goal or goals should be broad in scope and identify the abstract purpose of the policy or program that the committee will develop. An objective, however, is explicit and measurable. As Welsh and Harris (2016) note, "Objectives should define clearly and concisely exactly what outcome is to be achieved by the intervention" (p. 91). Each objective should have a time frame, a target population, a result, and a criterion by which success can be measured. The objectives should also be attainable and reasonable.

It is important to set ambitious goals and objectives, but at the same time, they must be achievable so as not to set up the committee or the policy/ program for failure. Educators often have high goals for themselves and their students, but do not forget that you are not trying to eradicate violence overnight, but rather to reduce it over time.

The goals and objectives should be firmly based on the description of the problem and pertinent information. The goals should address the problem directly; the measurable aspects of the objectives should focus on reducing events by observing trends and responding to them accordingly. Lastly, the committee should focus on the unit of analysis. One goal may address schoolwide issues, such as climate and attitudes, while another goal may focus on individual units of analysis, such as students, events, or teachers. Then, the corresponding objectives align with those goals.

Perhaps the most important issue in creating goals is ensuring that they align with the values of the school (as represented by the committee), and that they are fair, reasonable, and directly related to the problem. Everyone on the committee should agree that the stated goals are important, meaning-ful, and relevant to the school community.

As an example of goal and objective setting for a committee choosing to address the issues of fistfights, the members may have found that there is an attitude of support for such violence among students, and that the fights have been increasing each year with a record 35 in the past school year. Examples of goals and objectives may be found in table 5.2.

Note that the goals that the committee develops are specifically related to the individual aspects of the problem, but remain broad and abstract. The objectives, however, align with the goals and their unit of analysis (school-wide vs. individuals or events), and they have measurable outcomes, time frames, and criteria.

Table 5.2.   Examples of Problem-Oriented Goals and Objectives

Problem: School climate	Goal: To decrease student support for student violence	Objective 1: Decrease attitudinal support among all students by 20% in one year as measured by an attitudes survey
		Objective 2: Increase positivity for nonviolent conflict resolution by 10% in one year as measured by an attitudes survey
Problem: Excessive fights	Goal: To reduce the severity and occurrences of fistfights between students	Objective 1: Reduce the number of fistfights by 30% in one year as measured by discipline reports
		Objective 2: Reduce the number of student injuries by 40% in one year as measured by nurse's office reports and discipline reports

Step 4: Choose a Theory

Once the committee has agreed on common goals and values, members must choose a theoretical framework with which to view the problem. As chapter 1 explains, the criminological theories serve as the foundation on which effective policies and programs are built. They essentially provide a rationale for the solution while addressing specific mechanisms and processes by which the problem occurs.

If you refer back to the theories offered in the first chapter, you will note the differences in the fundamental explanations for violence. Strong programs will aim to address your problem analysis and view the issue through the lens of one or more theories. If the theories in this book are insufficient, there are other psychological and sociological theories on which you can develop a problem. Regardless of which you use, the program or policy (as drawn out in step 5 through the impact model) will address the components of theory that drive the problem and aim to improve or eradicate the problem. In choosing a theory-driven policy, you will create a step-by-step way to acknowledge these issues in order to achieve the goals and objectives that you have outlined.

A simple example of theory-driven policy in criminal justice programming and planning can be found using one of the most commonly utilized theories in modern criminology. Developed by Felson and Cohen (1980), routine activities theory (not included in chapter 1) explains that certain environments and conditions create circumstances that make criminality likely. The authors specifically outline that "direct-contact predatory violations require the convergence in space and time of *offenders, suitable targets*, and *the absence of effective guardians*" (Felson & Cohen, 1980, p. 389), and the model is shown in figure 5.1.

The theory's practical implication in policing involves target hardening through security measures such alarm systems, or increased guardianship through frequent police patrols and surveillance cameras. By using this theory to address real-world problems, police, business, and citizens can address one specific component of the problem to create a prevention method. In the example of student-on-student school violence, offenders are the students who engage in the violence, suitable targets are the victims of the violence, and the effective guardians are mostly teachers and school employees.

A theory-driven program, then, would use this theory to address one or more aspects of the model. By increasing effective guardianship either through teacher training or enhanced staff presence in student-dense areas, it would reduce the likelihood of crime or violence in schools.

In preparation for this meeting, members should have read and evaluated the theories presented in this book (and potentially others) to explain the problem. They also should have considered the problem analysis (including the history of the problem) and decided on a theory that they believe best explains the problem that the school faces. The meeting should then include a discussion about ways the theory fits your own particular school environment, and members can vote on the theoretical framework that they believe best suits the problem. The same meeting should focus on an impact model.

Step 5: Create an Impact Model

Those who create programs or conduct research often take the time to draw out depictions of their plans. Creating flowcharts, process models, cycles, or

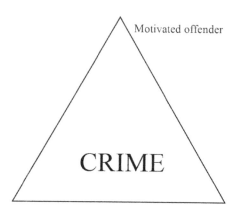

Figure 5.1.   Routine activities theory.

other illustrations to outline their logic and thinking helps organize the information and ways to address a problem. A strong impact model will demonstrate how a theory relates to a problem, and will in turn drive the plan. The components of your plan should be clearly related, as evidenced by your problem analysis. Remember that the theoretical components are the beams that holds up the problem, and your plans should be intended to remove or damage the beams in order to collapse the issue or, at the very least, put a dent in it.

As Welsh and Harris (2016) explain, and impact model is

> a prediction that a particular intervention will bring about a specific change in the problem. Formulating such a model forces us to answer several important questions: What is the intervention? Why would we expect a proposed intervention to work? Which causes of the problem will it address? In other words, through what process will change occur, and why? What outcome (a change in the problem) is expected? (p. 95)

By drawing out the elements of the theory and the expected change (through the goals and the objectives), your committee will clearly be able to observe ways to address the problem and create a plan that speaks directly to the theoretical pieces of the violence puzzle.

Figure 5.2 depicts the first three stages of the impact model using the school climate and physical violence problems, goals, and objectives from table 5.2. The figure shows the components of social bond theory and posits that a breakdown in those elements of the bonds leads to the problems that were voted on and defined by the committee. The theory explains that attachment, commitment, belief, and involvement in a child's life generates conforming and rule-abiding behavior. This can occur in communities, families, and schools. However, in the absence of these elements, or when there are weakened social bonds, it can lead to a school climate that celebrates aggression and violence and excessive fighting between students.

When the impact model is drawn out in this way, the clear response for a program or policy is to find ways to enhance social bonds through these four elements. An effective plan could be universal, targeted, or intensive (depending on which of the two problems it aims to address), but it would address ways to develop these parts of the social bond theory and therefore, reduce the violence issues.

Once the committee has drawn out the beginning and the end of the impact model, the third piece is the intervention. The discussion of ideas for the program or policy should be open and conversational. Committee members should feel free to be honest and idealistic, provided that their notions relate directly to the elements of the theory. This portion of the meeting should truly be focused on brainstorming ways to bring about theory-driven change and allow for the creativity and ingenuity of the members to shine.

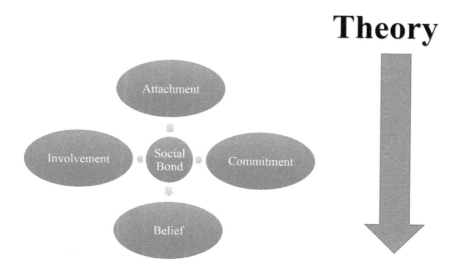

Figure 5.2. Social bond theory and problem impact model.

The result of this meeting is the beginning of the impact model and a hodgepodge of ideas that, organized and implemented correctly, may be the solution to the problem and the means by which the goals and objectives can be achieved. The members should leave this meeting thinking about organized, step-by-step ways to make these ideas work and how they would look in the context of the school environment.

Step 6: Plan

The fifth meeting to address step 6 is the nuts-and-bolts meeting. This is where the committee gathers to plan and organize the ideas created during the brainstorming session. Prior to this meeting, members should have prepared a basic outline of what a program or policy would look like and ways that it could be delivered effectively to the target population. While not every plan or idea will be implemented, this collaborative process aims to take the best ideas from everyone on the committee, combine/use them, and create the best possible intervention to address the problem.

With the impact model clearly displayed, the committee members should come together to share their ideas, and then go to work to create their own program. They should identify the pieces of the individual plans they like the most and discuss ways to implement them. While this does not need to start out with overly specific measures, the committee will eventually create a step-by-step outline of how the program will work. Remember that all the steps should be firmly rooted in theory and the impact model to specifically address the goals and objectives.

Once the outline has been created, the committee needs to identify the most specific ways that this program will work. The entire plan must clearly explain who will receive the intervention, who will deliver the intervention, in what order the program will occur, and how much and how often the intervention will occur.

First, the program must explain the target population. Will this address individuals through a targeted or intensive approach, or the entire school community via a universal intervention? If a specific, targeted population is the goal, the committee must decide on the criteria for eligibility in the program. Referring back to the sample goal of reducing fistfights, perhaps the committee would choose to focus on students who have had angry outbursts in the past three months. They could use counselor referrals and discipline reports to determine this, and use a specific checklist for inclusion criteria.

Additionally, the committee needs to specifically identify the number of students that the program can serve. How many students can a targeted or intensive intervention serve before the program grows too large and results in minimal or diminishing returns?

Next, the focus should be on the delivery. Who will be responsible for providing these services, activities, or duties? In times when most school employees feel overwhelmed with responsibilities and important issues, it may be best to consider existing resources as potential providers. When people create programs from scratch, they often overlook people, offices, or programs that already exist to serve a specific purpose. Collaboration and utilization of these resources is important in reducing workload and evenly distributing responsibility and tasks. A strong program does not simply implement an intervention, but it also encourages collaboration and partnership in a coordinated, planned effort.

In addition to identifying those responsible for program implementation, it is also necessary to include the steps for any planning and preparation. These, too, should include the responsible party. For both the steps of the program and the preparation, the committee should outline specific dates by which these tasks should be completed to stay on track with their implementation.

As an added measure, the plan should include ways to elicit buy-in from stakeholders. How will you include parents, community members, school staff and faculty, and students? What methods will be used to generate excitement and participation in this program or intervention? While the committee members may be enthusiastic about the plan, others may not share in their hopefulness and excitement. The program should include ways to not only justify the program, but also generate support and interest in it.

Lastly, the plan needs to be explicit about the order of the program as well as the frequency and the dosage. For example, if the target population is going to participate in anger management meetings, the committee needs to clearly explain how often these meetings will occur, the duration of the meetings, and the date when the meetings will cease.

This process seems daunting, and in reality, there are many components of this planning that the committee needs to lay out clearly. It may be useful to use a Gantt chart to organize, schedule, and plan the information. With many free templates available online, a Gantt chart provides a clear visual for the committee members by using a bar chart to show time intervals and tasks to be completed. Table 5.3 also provides a graphic organizer for the committee to use to organize the provisions and the procedures of the program and planning.

Once the committee has completed these steps, the meeting can adjourn, and the members should take time afterward to review it for concerns, problems, and unintended consequences. What, if any, could be the worst-case scenario at each step, and is that scenario manageable or minimal enough to make the implementation of the program still feasible?

Also, committee members should be sure that the program is developmentally and age appropriate. It would also be helpful at this time for some members to informally discuss this with other school community members, including the ad hoc members, union representatives, other administrators, and students. This is an ideal time for feedback, consideration, and buy-in from stakeholders.

The informal discussion may allow for further reflection and discussion of considerations or consequences that the members of the committee may

Table 5.3. Graphic Organizer for Planning

Action	Responsible parties	Start Date	Frequency (if applicable)	End Date	Cost	Actionable Items

not have addressed. Committee members should share their reflections or ideas via email before the next meeting, and the committee can discuss adjustments, edits, and changes at the start of the next meeting.

Lastly, in reading through the plan again, each committee member should be sure that the plans are clear enough that they could be read and conducted by a non-committee member. This allows for clarity and a clear implementation process. If there is confusion at any step, this needs to be addressed to head off potential problems in the future.

Step 7: Monitor

Once the program or policy has been developed, and the committee and the responsible parties begin to implement the plan, it becomes important to monitor the ways in which it progresses. First, the committee members should take time to ensure that each step is working as it was intended, and is able to progress to the next sequential step in the program. While the steps have been planned and coordinated meticulously, it is also important for the committee to make adjustments to make elements of the program as effective as possible.

Additionally, the committee should monitor the data and ensure that it is showing improvement and being collected accurately. If, for example, the committee is using discipline reports to monitor the number of physical confrontations, it should ensure that all administrators continue to use the same definition and manner of filing the reports. The committee can also monitor weekly or monthly progress to track trends and patterns over time.

Step 8: Evaluate Outcomes

Once the program has reached its natural and planned conclusion, the penultimate task is to evaluate the outcomes. Referring back to the objectives, this is the time to evaluate the effectiveness of the program or policy. Using descriptive statistics and other available data, it is important to identify program outcomes and decide if the program was, in fact, successful.

Additionally, it is important to disaggregate the data to see if the program was successful not only for the entire target population but also for smaller groups. The committee can and should examine the data to compare outcomes between, for example, male and female students, or minority and white students. This ensures that there is equity in the program and, if there are differences, it will allow the committee to make adjustments aimed at helping all students.

Step 9: Reassess and Review

The last step of the process allows the committee to decide if it would like to restart the program or repeat it in coming years. Obviously, if the program or policy was successful, it should be repeated or re-implemented. If it was not, or if the plan did not achieve the desired objectives, the members of the committee should determine how and why it failed.

This meeting should be an honest, yet respectful discussion about components of the program that can be improved, ways that the implementation and process may not have matched the intended plan, and consequences or effects that the committee may not have been able to foresee. If the program came close to achieving its goals and objectives, this is the time to review and edit the plan in order to repeat and aim for increased or improved results. It may be that the committee created goals that were too lofty or ambitious, or it may require a reflection on the impact model, the implementation, and the responsible parties.

If the committee decides to evaluate, adjust, and re-implement, or continue the program or policy, members should start back at step 4 and examine the theory and logic, and then continue the steps again. This allows for constant development of the program or policy and an assurance that it will continue to evolve and grow as the target population changes.

CONCLUSION

This chapter provided the steps necessary for practical application of the information provided in this book, combined with your own years of knowledge of education. By using a collaborative model to create theoretically sound, evidence-based practices, this process allows educators to create a program to address specific problems that are unique in their own causes, histories, and manifestations.

While there are effective programs that have specifically been designed for universal, targeted, and intensive interventions, schools and school employees often have the necessary resources to address the problems on their own. With a strong commitment to solving the problem and an investment of time, energy, and effort, school employees can demonstrate their own talent, creativity, and most importantly, their commitment to school safety.

As a final word, note that schools are not in this journey alone. The responsibilities and demands are often overwhelming, but without a doubt, there are opportunities for collaboration and support in communities. Colleges and universities can be helpful to schools in that they are nearly always open to opportunities for partnerships for research and service. Education, sociology, psychology, and criminology departments often hope to engage in research opportunities and evaluation, but are sometimes met with closed doors at schools.

Researchers and professors are generally not seeking to "catch" schools and school administrators in wrongdoing. Rather, they are hoping to help find empirically based practices to better serve students and keep school staff safe and secure so that learning can take place. If schools are willing to form partnerships with college and university faculty, this can create important bonds between community institutions and alleviate the heavy burden of responsibility involved in policy and program implementation and evaluation.

NOTE

1. https://www.nasponline.org
2. https://www.edjj.org
3. For more evaluations of PBIS, see Bradshaw, Koth, Bevans, Ialongo, & Leaf (2008), Bradshaw, Waasdorp, & Leaf (2012), and Horner, Sugai, Smolkowski, Todd, Nakasato, & Esperanza (2009).
4. The National Center on Intensive Intervention at American Institutes for Research is funded by the U.S. Department of Education's Office of Special Education Programs. Information can be found at https://intensiveintervention.org/.

Chapter Six

On School Shootings

We can't tolerate this anymore. These tragedies must end. And to end them, we must change.

—Barack Obama

From Colorado to Georgia to California to Alaska, schools have been a target for symbolic violence against random children. More often than not, the perpetrators of school shootings are students who attended or formerly attended the institution and seek revenge or a final act of strength against peers who mocked them or overlooked them (Daly, 2017). The problem is not new, and many fail to note that school shootings occurred even before the attack at Columbine High School in 1999.

The problem, though, is twofold. First, there are members of our society who see their best course of action as large-scale violence and revenge. They experience threats to their masculinity, social and academic failure, or tragedy, and their response is to take up weapons with the intention of murdering children and teenagers.

Secondly, the sense of safety in schools has been shaken to the core. If children are not safe in schools, how can anyone be safe anywhere? As noted in chapter 3, however, thousands of children in America have been scared for years. From bullying to fistfights to shootings, fear in schools is not new, but right now there is a simmering desire for change because, frankly, everyone has had it with senseless tragedies.

Like nationwide crime rates, aggregate rates of school violence and crime have been decreasing steadily since the 1990s, but the perception is that crime in schools is increasing (Musu-Gillette, Zhang, Wang, Zhang, & Oudekerk, 2017). This is partly due to widely publicized acts of violence and constant coverage of news stories. This is, however, a time when rates of fear at school are rising for all students, including those in rich and poor schools, and in black, brown, and white communities.

LARGE- AND SMALL-SCALE VIOLENCE: REVISITING THE THEORIES

It is difficult to compare rampage-type school shootings with gang- and poverty-related violence in urban areas. But though they have profoundly different root causes, the criminological theories discussed in chapter 2 remain constant. Strain theory, as it applies to school shooters, asserts that violence occurs when an individual faces stressors or negative life experiences that affect his ability to achieve socially accepted goals.

For school shooters, it may be a marked lack of friends (though many shooters had at least one friend), failed romantic relationships, or academic inadequacy. School shooters often experience social marginalization and individual vulnerabilities (Newman, Fox, Harding, Mehta, & Roth, 2005), such as mental illness or troubling family lives.

Similarly, most school shooters had weakened or diminished social bonds. They may not have believed in common goals, nor did they feel attached, committed, or involved in prosocial relationships or institutions. With deteriorated relationships and social prospects, revenge and large-scale violence may seem like a better, more viable option.

Finally, recall that routine activities required three specific elements in order for a crime to occur: a motivated offender, a suitable target, and a lack of capable guardianship. When discussing school safety in terms of prevention against mass shootings, some measures seem like common sense in a post-Columbine world. They focus on issues of capable guardianship and target hardening. Such measures include closed-circuit security cameras, metal detectors, armed officers, and secure entryways.

While these are certainly options to consider, research often shows (as discussed in chapter 3) that enhanced security measures often increase students' perceptions of fear. If such measures are to be implemented, they should be paired with supportive measures that aim to assist students and provide them with services.

TWO SUGGESTIONS FOR SCHOOLS

First and foremost, schools can create programs (through the stepped process outlined in chapter 5) to create stronger bonds with students. If it is an agreed-on problem that a small percentage of students are lonely or marginalized, schools can create ways to engage them in school activities. While such students may not necessarily become captain of the football team the following year, a small goal of creating a meaningful relationship with one adult or student may be helpful in providing a lifeline to a student who may not otherwise have one.

Unfortunately, most teachers, administrators, and even students can identify children who "fit the profile"[1] of a school shooter. If they do not use this terminology, they can at least answer the question, "If anyone were going to shoot people at school, who would it be?" While this is incredibly frightening, it also indicates that there are specific warning signs and subtle (or not-so-subtle) clues that are indicative of problematic behavior.

This would be a strong starting point for some type of outreach to a target population. As a word of (likely obvious) caution, it should not be made clear to these students that they are being selected for this specific reason, and every effort should be made to avoid singling them out in front of their peers, as this may exacerbate the situation.

Secondly, it may be helpful for all members of the school community, including parents, to have a better understanding of the warning signs. While most would be able to answer the aforementioned question, they would likely have a difficult time offering concrete reasons why they can identify a person. In order to avoid the simple "he gives me the creeps" responses, training programs in warning signs and processes may be of immense help. Organizations like Sandy Hook Promise[2] offer free programs with easy-to-implement curricula.

Programs include Know the Signs, Safety Assessment and Intervention, and Say Something. As Sandy Hook Promise notes on its website, "By building a culture of 'looking out for one another' and reporting possible threats when someone sees, reads, or hears something (especially within social media), entire communities and lives will be saved" (Sandy Hook Promise, 2018). For schools, this is a simple, cost-effective way to provide research-based training and assistance to students and communities to implement immediate training.

With the additional but necessary burden of school security debates, school employees need to consider the importance of time constraints. As many employees are already overburdened and overwhelmed, adding more to their plates seems impossible. Given the known warning signs, school employees need the time and availability to notice, recognize, and address these signs. With discussions about school safety measures that will literally cost tens (if not hundreds) of thousands of dollars, there should also be additional discussion about adding support services.

If schools can discuss finding money for training programs to arm teachers, we can certainly have discussions about adding more mental health services in school (and the latter does not involve more weapons in schools). Additional counselors and support staff, especially ones who are trained in recognizing warning signs, will have a net gain in any environment. They would have more time to meet with students, especially those who are often overlooked or fade into the background.

The American School Counselor Association (2018) recommends a 250-to-1 student-to-counselor ratio. The national average is 491-to-1, and only three U.S. states fall below the average recommendation. In the absence of violence, there is still a net gain with more counselors and a lighter caseload. They would still work to help all students, and have more time to promote prosocial behaviors and academic success. Addressing these issues with younger children ensures healthy development and lessens the likelihood of violence in the future.

Though this chapter was brief, the aim was to apply criminological theories to school shootings and offer two simple, but theory-driven approaches to prevention. The national- and state-level debates will undoubtedly continue, but there are immediate actions that can be taken to make a small but potentially meaningful change.

NOTES

1. Note that there is no clear profile of a school shooter, but there are common themes that the Secret Service found in an in-depth, qualitative study of shooters. More information can be found in the U.S. Secret Service and U.S. Department of Education (2004) *Final Report and Findings of the Safe School Initiative* at https://www2.ed.gov/admins/lead/safety/preventingattacksreport.pdf.

2. For more information, visit sandyhookpromise.org or search for the Sandy Hook Promise Facebook group to become a Promise Leader.

Conclusion

Where We Go from Here

Addressing school violence in a meaningful way requires that educators at all levels engage in a thorough examination of the theoretical roots of aggression and have an understanding of the scope and frequency of the problems and the effects of school violence. From there, teachers, administrators, and others can reflect on their own experiences and emotions, create their own plans and approaches, and work with a team to create tailored, specific programs to address their school's unique problems.

After working with children for years (or decades), it sometimes becomes difficult to remember that they are products of their own environment and individual development. The neurological, development, and psychological research all consistently agree that children and teenagers function at a profoundly different level than adults, and it affects the ways they think through problems, examine consequences, and consider short- and long-term gratification.

It also becomes important to recall these differences when applying criminological theories to issues of school-related violence. Theories including deterrence, strain, social learning, and social bond are even more interesting when examined in the context of adolescent development and children. Combined with notions of personal fables and imaginary audiences, it is not hard to imagine why many children and teenagers struggle with behavior and following rules.

National data and statistics can provide figures on exactly how many students experience violence (either as victims, offenders, or both), and these data can serve as a baseline for comparison to your individual school. This is a strong starting place for schools as you set out to conduct your own problem analyses and attempt to address problems that affect your students and faculty.

There are often obstacles and challenges to this process, either due to issues of research methodology, consent, or self-reporting. Remember that this is not a problem that you must address alone. Partnerships with colleges, nonprofit organizations, and other institutions can serve as a vital tool for completing these exercises and conducting your own studies.

Statistics show that thousands of children experience threats, thefts, and assaults at school, and even those students who are perpetrators are at risk for negative short- and long-term effects. One of the goals of education is to protect all students and provide them with the skills that they need. Knowing the consequences of violence in school—for both victims and offenders—the stakes are incredibly high for all students.

Students who are afraid of victimization at school are at an increased likelihood of depression, anxiety, decreased academic functioning, and absenteeism, while those who are misbehaving and receiving punitive consequences are far more likely to become a part of the school-to-prison pipeline, among other effects.

Additionally, the effects of violence are not limited to students. Teachers are affected by violence, too, and their perceptions of fear are directly related to levels of disengagement, burnout, and turnover. Especially in high-risk schools, where social bonds matter most, teacher turnover can be incredibly detrimental to the school and the students.

Ultimately, you are the person who decides what role you play in the violence and the solution. Chapter 4 asked you to examine your own limitations and willingness to intervene when confronted with violence. Because violence typically occurs quickly, the chapter offers solutions to slowing down the buildup before it occurs, and also asked you to prepare yourself for what will happen if and when you are faced with physical violence.

By preparing yourself in much the same way that you would practice a fire drill, your level of preparation can affect your decisions and actions in future interactions with students. The best-case scenario, obviously, is that you would be able to prevent violence before it occurs (for your own sake and for the students), but in the event that the situation escalates quickly, you need to know decisions that you will make, especially in the context of other colleagues.

In addition to addressing your own skills, limitations, and actions, you can also work together with your peers to evaluate the larger problems that your school faces, identify the scope and frequency of the problem, and create a theory-based, data-driven program specifically designed to address the students (or another population) in your school. Using the resources and the steps outlined in chapter 5, schools can create large- or small-scale approaches and interventions with clear, measurable goals and objectives.

And finally, while the book was not intended to address school shootings, the strategies in chapter 5 can also be used to address school safety and prevention of such issues. By highlighting marginalized students as a problem, schools (and particularly support services) can identify at-risk students, ensure that they address strains, and work to restore social bonds. Also, you can implement free programs through Sandy Hook Promise that are designed to acknowledge and create awareness about warning signs while also supporting students, teachers, and parents.

The problems that schools and students are facing today are broad in scope and multifaceted, but there are structured, evidence-based ways to address them. By using a systematic, multidisciplinary approach to reducing common, everyday violence, teachers, counselors, administrators, and others can work to protect and help all students by interrupting the school-to-prison pipeline, focusing on rehabilitation and restoration, and creating tailored, unique programs to address school-specific problems.

Schools and school employees cannot be expected to solve these problems alone, but they also cannot wait for politicians and legislators to save them with funding and programming. Instead, you can implement small changes that restore relationships with students, prevent violence before it occurs, and ensure that schools become the safe havens that they used to be.

Through it all, it is imperative that you remember that this is a job that is important, meaningful, and absolutely necessary. Your commitment to children and their futures is one that is noble, and in the face of additional threats to your safety and that of your students, know that you are appreciated and valued. Thank you for everything that you do. Thank you for working every day to ensure that the future is in good hands.

Appendix A

How Would You Handle a Violence Scenario?

Read the following scenarios and describe the situational and student factors that may affect your decisions. Examine your plan and identify moments when you could intervene to prevent the physical violence, or what you would do while it is happening.

SCENARIO

During lunch in the cafeteria, two large female high school students in the middle of the room engage in a verbal argument while seated at the table. Their voices begin to get louder as they start to curse and threaten each other. They stand up quickly, knocking over chairs. They are standing nose to nose, yelling at each other, when one pushes the other.

The student who was pushed, Student B, quickly reacts by punching Student A in the face. The students at the table with the girls and at nearby tables begin to crowd around as they pull out their phones to record. They cheer as other students from the cafeteria run to see what is happening. The two girls are now scuffling on the floor getting in punches whenever possible. The crowd around them now restricts the ability of school resource officers to intervene.

Which factors did you identify as affecting your decisions?

SCENARIO (ANNOTATED)

During lunch in the *cafeteria* (1), *two large female high school students* (2) in *the middle of the room* (3) engage in a verbal argument while seated at the table. Their voices begin to get louder as they start to *curse and threaten* (4) each other. They stand up quickly, *knocking over chairs* (5). They are standing *nose to nose, yelling* (6) at each other, when one *pushes* (7) the other.

The student who was pushed, Student B, *quickly reacts by punching Student A in the face* (8). The students at the table with the girls and at nearby tables begin to *crowd around* (9) as they *pull out their phones* (10) to record. They cheer as *other students* (11) from the cafeteria run to see what is happening. The two girls are now scuffling *on the floor* (12) getting in punches whenever possible. The *crowd* (13) around them now restricts the ability of school resource officers to intervene.

1. *Location in school*: The cafeteria—in addition to other areas such as locker rooms, bathrooms, and bus loading areas—is a common location for student conflicts. Either due to lack of supervision and support or a high faculty-to-student ratio, this may affect how safe (or unsafe) you perceive the situation to be. Behre, Astor, and Meyer (2001) found that middle school teachers

were more likely to change their response to and intervene in a fight if it occurred in their classroom as compared to non-classroom locations.

2. *Gender, age, and size of students:* Students' gender, age, and size can affect your own decisions to intervene. Often, male employees feel hesitant to intervene in a fight with female students for fear of being perceived as inappropriately touching the students. Similarly, female employees may be intimidated by larger students who may potentially overpower them in an altercation.

As the students in this scenario are high school students, they are likely larger and stronger than elementary or middle school students, which may also affect decisions. In the early results of a study, Daly (in progress) found that teachers and school employees listed the size and gender of the students fighting as two of the top five reasons (of 11 options) that affect their decision to intervene.

3. *Proximity and location*: Often, when monitoring larger areas such as the cafeteria, teachers and other employees tend to stand around the perimeter of the location. Because, in this scenario, the participants in the conflict are in the center of the room, employees would need to move closer to the situation in order to de-escalate it. Given the swift nature of fights, this could essentially be the difference between talking students down or having to break up a physical fight. Those charged with monitoring students should consider walking through the center of the room or moving around the area in order to maintain proximity to more students and increase the likelihood that they might be closer to a conflict if and when it occurs.

4. *Tension and attention-grabbing*: In this moment, the students are (either intentionally or unintentionally) drawing attention to themselves. This is also increasing the likelihood of and need for violence, as the students must save face and maintain their reputations in the face of disrespect. During this buildup of tension, this is the final opportunity to intervene and de-escalate the situation before it becomes physical. If you have the opportunity to separate the students and talk to each of them quietly and calmly (without the ever-important audience of their peers), you can avoid the physical conflict.

5. *Physical situation*: Once the students stand up (and subsequently knock over furniture), the situation has now become incredibly tense. Through posturing and physicality, the students have continued to call attention to themselves and are staged to engage in what will likely be a physical fight. It now requires more skill (and risk) for you to enter the situation and de-escalate the conflict. This necessitates your own decision and physical ability to stand between the girls to talk to them or move them away from each other. Had you not been paying attention to the yelling in the moments before this, you would have come upon this situation and essentially been too late to address the situation without physicality.

6. *Buildup and proximity of students*: While they have not engaged in physical contact yet, their proximity (being nose to nose) and their behavior (yelling at each other) is continuing the buildup of tension. And as they are so close to each other, the likelihood of violence is high. To de-escalate the situation now, you would likely need to touch the students in order to separate them (with at least a hand on the arm or shoulder), making this situation even more tense.

7. *More serious physical contact*: Once a student has initiated physical contact with another, this becomes a more serious situation. By pushing her, Student A has now required that Student B retaliate with similar or greater force. Though Student B may not have wanted to fight or continue the conflict, Student A has both physically and symbolically pushed Student B to respond.

8. *Increased physical contact*: Student B has now responded accordingly, and this tense situation has officially become a fistfight. At this point, you may be inclined to remove yourself from the situation completely out of fear of injury to yourself or to the students. If you have already decided that you are absolutely unwilling to enter a situation in which students are engaged in violence, you then become a third-party employee who has a different role. You must, in this situation, find another way to end the fight, either through calling for assistance or moving students out of the way.

9. *Bystander gathering*: Now the third-party bystanders play a crucial role. The nearby students are not only egging on the students and continuing the buildup of tension, but by gathering around the girls, they are calling even more attention to the situation. Their support of their friends also encourages the violence and can present the threat of an even larger conflict if they choose to engage in the physical violence.

10. *Presentation of video recording*: Once students begin to gather around and are excited for a fight, they typically use their phones to record the action. Such easy access to technology serves to document the excitement and provides fodder for future discussions about the altercation. This is almost an instinctive response for the students, and it presents the need for further consideration for employees who may intervene. Video documentation of their actions may pose an added threat, and it should be a part of your decision-making process.

11. *Gathering of a larger crowd*: Now, in addition to the select group of students who were in close proximity to the girls, other students in the cafeteria are running closer to the fight. Their added influence and excitement contributes to what Collins (2009, 2013) calls the "tunnel of violence." As he explains:

> the non-participating part of the crowd is not superfluous. They provide a
> necessary backdrop to the small clusters of violent activists, by cheering or

otherwise just making noise; they provide the emotional support that enables the violent elite to keep up their emotional energy. The crowd creates an emotional space, the center of which is occupied by the [participants]. They are the center of attention, and know that they are. (Collins, 2013, p. 143)

As such, their support enables the fight, and their encouragement and cheering will prolong the incident. In addition to addressing the girls who are fighting, teachers, administrators, and school security officers must now address the bystanders and disperse the crowd.

12. *Change of pace in the conflict*: Since the participants in the fight have now moved to the floor, the altercation becomes even more difficult. In order to intervene, employees must engage in physicality to remove the participants from the fight. This situation requires the adults to take a physical stance in which they may be off-balance or have less physical strength as compared to a standing position.

13. *Third-party inciters and their behavior*: By this point, if more employees are present or school resource officers and administrators have arrived to address the conflict, the crowd that has gathered around the fight can hinder access to the participants. Those who are specifically charged with breaking up the fight now have the added task of moving students out of the way and making a path into the center of the crowd. The incident has created a large-scale disruption in the cafeteria, and it will likely continue throughout the day and affect learning.

Appendix B

Indicators of School Crime and Safety

As a joint publication of the Bureau of Justice Statistics and the National Center for Education Statistics, the yearly *Indicators of School Crime and Safety* report compiles data from a variety of sources. As noted in chapter 2, the publication offers data from the School-Associated Violent Death Surveillance System, the Department of Justice, the Center for Disease Control and Prevention, the National Crime Victimization Survey and School Crime Supplement, and others.

The report provides an important overview of aggregate, nationwide data from large-scale, methodologically sound surveys, but it also provides disaggregated data including differences based on gender, age, and race/ethnicity. Further, these indicators and the data that represent them offer a baseline to which you can compare your own school. If you find any of these indicators to be a concern in your school, you can access the document online, examine the ways that overall school violence was conceptualized and operationalized, and then compare your results to the national findings. This is a good place to start before convening a School Safety Committee meeting.

Violent Deaths

• Indicator 1: Violent deaths at school and away from school

Nonfatal Student and Teacher Victimization

• Indicator 2: Incidence of victimization at school and away from school
• Indicator 3: Prevalence of victimization at school
• Indicator 4: Threats and injuries with weapons on school property
• Indicator 5: Teachers threatened with injury or physically attacked by students

School Environment

• Indicator 6: Violence and other criminal incidents at public schools, and those reported to the police
• Indicator 7: Discipline problems reported by public schools
• Indicator 8: Students' reports of gangs at school
• Indicator 9: Illegal drug availability and drug-related discipline incidents
• Indicator 10: Students' reports of being called hate-related words and seeing hate-related graffiti
• Indicator 11: Bullying at school and cyber-bullying anywhere
• Indicator 12: Teachers' reports on school conditions

Fights, Weapons, and Illegal Substances

- Indicator 13: Physical fights on school property and anywhere
- Indicator 14: Students carrying weapons on school property and anywhere and students' access to firearms
- Indicator 15: Students' use of alcohol and alcohol-related discipline incidents
- Indicator 16: Students' use of marijuana

Fear and Avoidance

- Indicator 17: Students' perceptions of personal safety at school and away from school
- Indicator 18: Students' reports of avoiding school activities of classes or specific places in school

Discipline, Safety, and Security Measures

- Indicator 19: Serious disciplinary actions taken by public schools
- Indicator 20: Safety and security measures taken by public schools
- Indicator 21: Students' reports of safety and security measures observed at school

Postsecondary Campus Safety and Security

- Indicator 22: Criminal incidents at postsecondary institutions
- Indicator 23: Hate crime incidents at postsecondary institutions

The most recent publication of Indicators of School Crime and Safety can be found at https://nces.ed.gov/pubs2017/2017064.pdf.

Appendix C

Addressing the Cradle-to-Prison Pipeline

The impassioned report, *America's Cradle to Prison Pipeline*, from the Children's Defense Fund (2007) outlines factors that affect the cradle-to-prison pipeline (and, in a related way, the school-to-prison pipeline), and highlights ways to make positive change that can happen immediately. Through research and case studies, the report provides an important wake-up call to parents, adults, schools, and communities for those who are interested.[1]

The report offers eight ways that "we come together and do the hard work to build a movement to save all our children and nation's soul" (Children's Defense Fund, 2007, p. 4). Though they are broad and potentially idealistic, they capture the root of the problem and explain ways that the work must begin:

1. Name and change the Pipeline and work tougher, recognizing that children do not come in pieces but in families and communities and are profoundly affected by the norms, priorities, policies, and values of our nation and culture.
2. Call and work for a fundamental paradigm shift in child policy and practice away from the too-frequent first choice of punishment and incarceration to prevention and early intervention and sustained child investment.
3. We must begin early by ensuring every child a healthy start through guaranteed comprehensive health and mental health coverage and coverage of pregnant women wherever they live in America.
4. Ensure quality Early Head Start, Head Start, child care, and preschool to get every child ready for school.
5. Link every child to a permanent, caring family member or adult mentor who can keep them on track and get them back on track if and when they stray.
6. Make sure every child can read by 4th grade and can graduate from school able to succeed at work and in life. An ethic of achievement and high expectations for every child must be created in every home, congregation, community, and school in our culture and public policies and practices.
7. Commit to helping the richest nation on earth end the child and family poverty that drives so much of the Pipeline process and the racial disparities faced by Black, Latino, and American Indian children who are disproportionately poor.
8. Dramatically decrease the number of children who enter the child welfare and juvenile and criminal justice systems, stop detaining children in adult jails, and reduce the racial disparities in these and other child serving systems. (Children's Defense Fund, 2007, pp. 4–6)

Further, the American Psychological Association Zero Tolerance Task Force provides a number of suggestions and recommendations for improving school practices and addressing the problems created by harsh, punitive policies.[2] The following are recommendations for reforming zero tolerance.

A.1.1. Apply zero tolerance policies with greater flexibility, taking school context and teacher expertise into account.

A.1.2. Teachers and other professional staff who have regular contact with students should be the first line of communication with parents and caregivers regarding disciplinary incidents.

A.1.3. Carefully define all infractions, whether major or minor, and train all staff in appropriate means of handling each infraction.

A.1.4. Evaluate all school discipline or school violence prevention strategies to ensure that disciplinary interventions, programs, or strategies are having a beneficial impact on student behavior and school safety.

A.2.1. Reserve zero tolerance disciplinary removals for only the most serious and severe of disruptive behaviors.

A.2.2. Replace one-size-fits-all disciplinary strategies with graduated systems of discipline, wherein consequences are geared to the seriousness of the infraction.

A.2.3. Require school police officers who work in schools to have training in adolescent development.

B.1.1. Implement preventative measures that can improve school climate and improve the sense of school community and belongingness.

B.1.2. Seek to reconnect alienated youth and reestablish the school bond for students at risk for disciplinary problems of violence. Use threat assessment procedures to identify the level of risk posed by student words.

B.1.3. Develop a planned continuum of effective alternatives for those students whose behavior threatens the discipline or safety of the school.

B.1.4. Improve collaboration and communication between schools, parents, law enforcement, juvenile justice, and mental health professionals in order to develop an array of alternatives for challenging youth. (American Psychological Association Zero Tolerance Task Force, 2008, pp. 857–859)

NOTES

1. To view the full report, visit http://www.childrensdefense.org/library/data/cradle-prison-pipeline-report-2007-full-highres.html.

2. For more information on findings and recommendations, see the full report, *Are Zero Tolerance Policies Effective in the Schools?* at http://www.apa.org/pubs/info/reports/zero-tolerance.pdf.

Appendix D

School Safety Committee Meeting Schedule

Meeting	Step	To do during the meeting	To do before next meeting
1	Step #1 Identify the problem	Discuss problems that affect behavior/learning Define problems using a uniform definition	Informally measure Ask questions Email findings
2	Step #2 Examine the scope and frequency	Choose problem on which to focus Decide about questions to ask and data necessary to answer Discuss the history of the problem	Collect data Try to explain patterns and trends Provide condensed history of the problem
3	Step #3 Set goals and objectives	Present about scope, frequency, and history Decide on goals and objectives (g/o) Complete g/o worksheet Decide on unit of analysis	Reflect on g/o Make adjustments or recommendations as necessary Read/review theoretical frameworks
4	Step #4 Choose a theory Step #5 Create an impact model	Discuss problem in the context of theoretical framework based on fit Vote on framework to use Develop an impact/logic model Brainstorm interventions, programs, and policies	Think about ways to organize and implement ideas Create an outline of program/policy
5	Step #6 Plan (Note: This will be the longest meeting. It can be broken up into two meetings if necessary.)	Create a program Apply best ideas and/or practices in a step-by-step outline Identify who will receive/deliver intervention, in what order, and how much/how often it will occur List stakeholders for buy-in Relate to g/o	Contact stakeholders and ensure buy-in Implement the program according the outline Informally check in with all parties involved to see how implementation goes Develop measurement tools
6	Step #7 Monitor	Ensure that program/policy is implemented as planned Evaluate data to be sure that it is being collected accurately	Continue informal monitoring Gather final data before next meeting
7	Step #8 Evaluate outcomes Step #9 Reassess and review	Analyze/evaluate data and compare to g/o Disaggregate data and compare within and between groups Decide if it was a success (based on g/o) Adjust and re-implement or abolish For adjustment, continue meetings from Step #5	

Appendix E

Questions to Ask about Problem Scope and Frequency

- Whom does the problem affect?
- Does the problem affect specific demographic groups differently?
- What percentage of students, teachers, and others are affected by the problem?
- Where does this problem most typically occur?
- At what times or on what days does the problem most typically occur?
- To what extent does this affect the learning environment?
- Why is the problem important?
- What are the short- and long-term effects?
- Which elements of the current policies to address the problem are ineffective?
- What are the contexts in which the problem occurs?
- How often does this affect teachers, students, and others?
- What is the financial cost of this problem?
- What is the social cost of the problem (e.g., missed classes, wasted time)?
- Has this problem increased or worsened over time?
- What has led to the changes in frequency of occurrence?
- Do similar schools or school districts have the same problem?
- How does this compare to national averages (as measured by the *Indicators of School Crime and Safety*)?

Appendix F

Impact Model Template

Appendix F

IMPACT MODEL 1

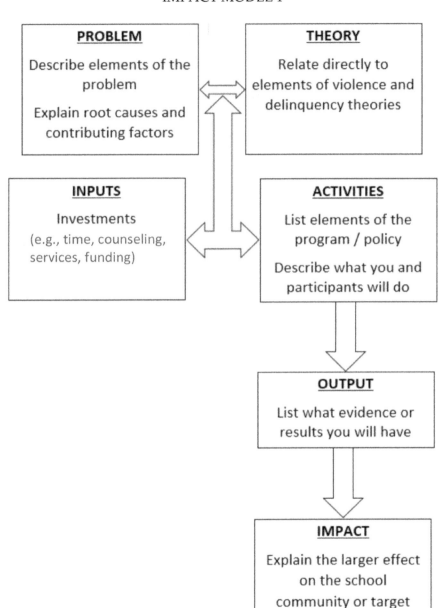

IMPACT MODEL 2

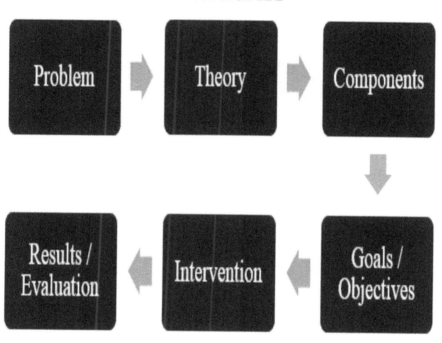

Appendix G

Sample Program Implementation Schedule

SAMPLE TUTORING/COUNSELING PROGRAM

Month(s)	Action(s)	Milestone(s)/Goals	Responsible Party
September	-identify -gather	-Identify target students -Gather initial baseline data	-School counselor -Vice principal
October	-counsel -tutor	-Create weekly counseling sessions -Provide after-school tutoring	-School counselor -English/LAL dept.
November	-collaborate -plan	-Meet with parents to discuss progress -Create short-term success strategy -Continue counseling and tutoring	-School counselor -Vice principal
December	-analyze -follow up -re-evaluate	-Analyze qualitative and quantitative data -Compare to initial goals -Discuss with stakeholders -Adjust and re-implement given feedback	-School counselor -Vice principal

SAMPLE AFTER-SCHOOL MENTORING PROGRAM

Month(s)	Action(s)	Milestone(s)/Goals	Responsible Party
September	-coordinate -plan	-Coordinate transportation and funding -Plan after-school activities (e.g., sports) -Plan snacks	-Vice principal -Athletic director -Food services
October	-promote -enroll -create	-Promote the program to student body -Enroll students during homeroom -Create measurement tools for objectives	-Athletic director -Student reps -School counselor
November	-measure -implement	-Assess student baseline data upon start. -Implement program 3x per week	-School counselor -Vice principal
February	-analyze -follow up -re-evaluate	-Interview students about program -Analyze qualitative and quantitative data -Compare to initial goals -Discuss with stakeholders -Adjust and re-implement given feedback	-School counselor -Vice principal -Athletic director

Appendix H

Sample Survey

Appendix H

The following survey was created as a part of a study of school employees' decisions to intervene in student conflicts. After the survey, the author provides a few specific aspects to note when creating your own survey.

1. **Gender**

   [ ] Male   [ ] Female   [ ] Choose to not answer

2. **Age**

   Please write your current age: _____   [ ] Choose to not answer

3. **Height**

   Feet: _____   Inches: _____   [ ] Choose to not answer

4. **Physical build**
   [ ] Slim/slender
   [ ] Athletic/toned
   [ ] Average
   [ ] Few extra pounds
   [ ] Stocky
   [ ] Overweight
   [ ] Unsure
   [ ] Choose to not answer

5. **Weight in pounds**

   Weight: _____   [ ] Choose to not answer

6. **Years teaching (total)**

   Years: _____   [ ] Choose to not answer

7. **Years at this current school**

   Years: _____   [ ] Choose to not answer

8. Job title

[ ] Teacher   If high school, list subject: _____
[ ] School Counselor
[ ] Administrator   List job title: _____
[ ] Social worker
[ ] School nurse
[ ] School security officer/resource officer
[ ] Teacher's aide/assistant/technician
[ ] Custodian
[ ] Other   List job title: _____

9. Race/Ethnicity (Check all that apply)

[ ] White
[ ] Hispanic/Latino
[ ] Black/African American
[ ] Native American or American Indian
[ ] Asian/Pacific Islander
[ ] Mixed race
[ ] Other   Please list: _____
[ ] Choose to not answer

10. Highest education level completed (If currently enrolled, check highest degree received)

[ ] No schooling completed
[ ] Preschool through 8th grade
[ ] Some high school, no diploma
[ ] High school graduate, diploma or the equivalent (e.g., GED)
[ ] Some college credit, no degree
[ ] Trade/technical/vocational training
[ ] Associate degree
[ ] Bachelor's degree
[ ] Master's degree
[ ] Professional degree
[ ] Doctoral degree
[ ] Choose to not answer

11. Physical limitations/disabilities (Check all that apply)

[ ] Physical disability
[ ] Intellectual or learning disability
[ ] Psychiatric disability
[ ] Visual impairment
[ ] Hearing impairment
[ ] Neurological disability
[ ] Choose to not answer

12. **Have you had any school violence prevention/reduction training during your teaching career?**

  [ ] Yes [ ] No

13. **Did you have any pre-service (pre-teaching/education) violence prevention/reduction training?**

  [ ] Yes [ ] No

14. **How important to you believe violence prevention/reduction training to be?**

  [ ] Extremely important
  [ ] Very important
  [ ] Moderately important
  [ ] Slightly important
  [ ] Not at all important

PERCEPTIONS OF SCHOOL & VIOLENCE

Directions: For question 15, please check one box per item/line expressing your satisfaction with each in terms of school safety.

15.

		Extremely Satisfied	Very Satisfied	Moderately Satisfied	Slightly Satisfied	Not at all Satisfied
a.	Overall satisfaction with the school in the past three years					
b.	Support from administrators					
c.	Support from peers					
d.	School safety measures					

Directions: For questions 16–17, please check one box for each item.

16. How often do you feel safe at work?

[ ] Always   [ ] Often   [ ] Sometimes   [ ] Seldom   [ ] Never

17. Has your own personal fear of violence or uneasiness caused any of the following?

		YES	NO
a.	Missed days of work		
b.	Required administrative intervention		
c.	Negative attitude about work		
d.	Become fearful of students		
e.	Poor relationships with peers		
f.	Poor relationships with students		
g.	Poor relationships with administrators		
h.	Avoiding particular areas in school		
i.	Avoiding particular students in school		
j.	Needed outside counseling/therapy		
k.	Warranted police intervention		
l.	Sought out other employment		
m.	Considered leaving the profession		
n.	Other (Please list in the space below)		

Appendix H

18. For the following problems, please list how often these problems seem to occur at your school.

		1	2	3	4	5
	1 = Never 2 = Rarely 3 = Sometimes 4 = Frequently 5 = Always					
a.	Grabbing, shoving					
b.	Punching, kicking					
c.	Stealing of personal property (no force used)					
d.	Physical threats					
e.	Cursing/profanity					
f.	Racial or ethnic personal insults					
g.	Fistfights					
h.	Cutting with sharp objects					
i.	Hitting with objects					
j.	Attacks requiring medical care					
k.	Personal property stolen by force					
l.	Intimidating by harassing					
m.	Gang intimidation					
n.	Drug use/sales in schools					
o.	Racial/ethnic conflicts					
p.	Car vandalism					
q.	Threatening with weapons (including guns)					
r.	Sexual attack					
s.	Shooting on or near campus					
t.	Homicide on or near campus					

Directions: For questions 19–20, please check one response per item/line.

19. How satisfied are you with the way that school administrators address student violence issues?

[ ] Extremely satisfied
[ ] Very satisfied
[ ] Moderately satisfied
[ ] Slightly satisfied
[ ] Not at all satisfied

20. Have you been a victim of any of the following by a student at your school?

		YES	NO
a.	Grabbing, shoving		
b.	Punching, kicking		
c.	Stealing of personal property (no force used)		
d.	Physical threats		
e.	Cursing/profanity		
f.	Racial or ethnic personal insults		
g.	Fistfights		
h.	Cutting with sharp objects		
i.	Hitting with objects		
j.	Attack requiring medical care		
k.	Personal property stolen by force		
l.	Intimidating by harassing		
m.	Gang intimidation		
n.	Car vandalism		
o.	Threatening with weapons (including guns)		
p.	Sexual attack		
q.	Shooting/attempted murder		

Questions 1–11 ask demographic questions about the survey respondent. This specific survey asks about physical characteristics to identify contributing factors that may affect a school employees' decision to intervene in physical violence. Obviously, if variables like height, physical build, disabilities, and weight, they can be omitted.

For demographic questions, though, it is important to ensure that the responses should be exhaustive (meaning they offer all possible responses) and mutually exclusive. For example, Question 9 asks the respondent to check all that apply in the event that they are bi- or multi-racial. These types of questions should provide adequate information so that you can compare results between specific groups such as gender, race, grade level (for students), and other characteristics. It may also be helpful for student respondents to indicate their vice-principal (in schools in which there is more than one), parental status (e.g. married, divorced, separated, single, etc.), and zip code (if students are coming from multiple areas). In other research areas, respondents are typically asked about income or socioeconomic status. Students, however, likely do not know this information, but zip codes may be a helpful indicator in the absence of family income information.

Questions 12 and 13 ask about participation in training or teaching preparation. By only offering yes or no options for responses, this allows for simple coding and comparison for descriptive statistics. Question 14 asks the employee respondent for their opinion about the importance of violence prevention/reduction training, and it offers a Likert-scale response ranging from extremely important to not important at all. These types of responses allow for a broader range of feelings and emotions, and for descriptive analysis after completion of the survey distribution, the mean and mode for responses provide important measures of central tendency among the staff members.

Question 15 also offers Likert-scale responses, but this time it provides a number of items measuring support and satisfaction. By providing these items in a matrix (or a table), it allows for easier reading and movement through the survey. When surveys are comprehensive (as they should be in order to gather as much data as possible), formatting tricks such as this one make the survey seem less tedious for the respondents.

Question 16 offers another Likert-scale response, although this refers to frequency of fear and uses a range of Always to Never. Question 17 remains consistent in the subject of fear and safety, and it asks if the subjects have ever caused any negative consequences. Again, through the use of a matrix, it allows for quick responses from the respondents, and it also offers them the opportunity to provide their own personal experience or negative outcome in the space marked "Other." This also ensures that the items are exhaustive and allow for all possible responses from the subjects.

Question 18 uses a Likert-scale temporal measure again to measure the employees' perceptions of how often they see these acts of violence at school. This is an important item on a survey, as it aims to measure perceptions of safety. While school administrators could easily identify the rates and frequency of each of these items per month (or per year), asking employees about their perception of them may highlight a discrepancy between actual and perceived rates.

Similarly, question 20 uses the same acts of violence to ask about victimization. As noted in chapter 3, prior teacher victimization can affect perceptions of violence and safety, which can, in turn, affect teacher engagement and effectiveness. This may also provide school administrators with a better sense of victimization rates in schools, even if the employees never reported the student behavior (for minor infractions like cursing or profanity). The same item could be used to measure student experiences as well. Students are less likely to report or even to be caught for such simple infractions, and a question like this on a survey could offer more insight about the rates at which these occur. In many ways, this is almost a better measure of some incidents as compared to official school discipline data, as directly asking about victimization captures even those cases which were not reported. In criminal justice research, this is often called "the dark figure of crime."

The questions on this survey were presented in this appendix to provide an overview of question types and responses in terms of efficiency, formatting, and descriptive statistics. Schools and school administrators can use similar questions and items in addition to creating their own to measure district-specific variables and problems.

As a reminder, you do not always need to recreate the wheel. Before attempting to create your own survey, a quick Google search may provide a pre-existing survey that has already been implemented and tested for issues of reliability and validity. As an example, searching for "school safety survey" yielded a result from the University of Nebraska–Lincoln's Student Engagement Project which offers surveys for elementary and secondary students, parents, and staff. These were field tested by academic researchers and offer scoring templates and PDF versions online. They can be found at https://k12engagement.unl.edu/the-safe-and-responsive-schools-safe-school-surveys.

References

Aber, J. L., Pedersen, S., Brown, J. L., Jones, S. M., & Gershoff, E. T. (2003). *Changing children's trajectories of development: Two-year evidence for the effectiveness of a school-based approach to violence prevention.* New York: National Center for Children in Poverty.

Agnew, R. (2006). *Pressured into crime: An overview of general strain.* Los Angeles: Roxbury Publishing Company.

Akers, R. L. (1998 [2011]). Social learning theory. Reprinted in F. T. Cullen & R. Agnew (Eds.), *Criminological theory: Past to present* (4th ed.) (pp. 140–153). New York: Oxford University Press.

Akiba, M. (2010). What predicts fear of school violence among U.S. adolescents? *Teachers College Record, 112*(1), 68–102.

American Psychological Association Zero Tolerance Task Force. (2008). Are zero tolerance policies effective in the schools? An evidentiary review and recommendations. *American Psychologist, 63*(9), 852–862.

American School Counselor Association. (2018). Press. Retrieved from https://www.schoolcounselor.org/press.

Baker, B. D., Farrie, D., & Sciarra, D. G. (2016). *Mind the gap: 20 years of progress and retrenchment in school funding and achievement gaps.* Policy Information Report, ETS Research Report Series ISSN 2330-8516.

Bandura, A. (1977). Social learning theory. Englewood Cliffs, NJ: Prentice Hall.

Beane, A., Miller, T. W., & Spurling, R. (2008). The Bully Free Program: A profile for prevention in the school setting. In T. W. Miller (Ed.), *School violence and primary prevention* (pp. 391–405). New York: Springer.

Beccaria, C. (1764). *An essay on crimes and punishments.* Reprinted 1872. Albany, NY: W. C. Little & Co. Retrieved from http://lf-oll.s3.amazonaws.com/titles/2193/Beccaria_1476_Bk.pdf.

Behre, W. J., Astor, R. A., & Meyer, H. A. (2001). Intervening in school violence: An examination of violence-prone school subcontexts. *Journal of Moral Education, 2*(30), 131–153.

Bosworth, K., Ford, L., & Hernandaz, D. (2011). School climate factors contributing to student and faculty perceptions of safety in select Arizona schools. *Journal of School Health, 81*(4), 194–201.

Bradshaw, C., Koth, C., Bevans, K., Ialongo, N., & Leaf, P. (2008). The impact of school-wide Positive Behavioral Interventions and Supports (PBIS) on the organizational health of elementary schools. *School Psychology Quarterly, 23*(4), 462–473.

Bradshaw, C., Waasdorp, T., & Leaf, P. (2012). Examining the variation in the impact of school-wide Positive Behavioral Interventions and Supports. *Pediatrics, 10*(5), 1136–1145.

Brief for Christopher Simmons as Amici Curiae Supporting Respondents, Roper v. Simmons, 543 US 551 (2005) (no. 03-633). Retrieved from: http://www.apa.org/about/offices/ogc/amicus/roper.pdf.

Burke, D. (2011). The growing wealth gap. *Fortune, 164*(7), 28–29.

Casey, B. J., Getz, S., & Galvan, A. (2008). The adolescent brain. *Developmental Review, 28*, 62–77.

Cauffman, E., & Steinberg, L. (2000). (Im)maturity and judgment in adolescence: Why adolescents may be less culpable than adults. *Behavioral Science & Law, 18*(6), 741–760.

Cedeno, L. A., Elias, M. J., Kelly, S., & Chu, B. C. (2010). School violence, adjustment, and the influence of hope on low-income, African American youth. *American Journal of Orthopsychiatry, 80*(2), 213–226.

Children's Defense Fund. (2007). *America's Cradle to Prison Pipeline*. Washington, DC: Children's Defense Fund. Retrieved from http://www.childrensdefense.org/library/data/cradle-prison-pipeline-report-2007-full-lowres.pdf.

Cohen, A. K. (1955). *Delinquent boys: The culture of the gang*. Glencoe, IL: Free Press.

Collins, R. (2013). Entering and leaving the tunnel of violence: Micro-sociological dynamics of emotional entrainment in violent interactions. *Current Sociology, 61*(2), 132–151.

Collins, R. (2009). *Violence: A micro-sociological theory*. Princeton, NJ: Princeton University Press.

Cooney, M. (1998). *Warriors and peacemakers: How third parties shape violence*. New York: NYU Press.

Cowan, K. C., Vaillancourt, K., Rossen, E., & Pollitt, K. (2013). *A framework for safe and successful schools* [brief]. Bethesda, MD: National Association of School Psychologists.

Cullen, F. T., & Agnew, R. (Eds.). (2011). *Criminological theory: Past to present* (4th ed.). New York: Oxford University Press.

Daly, S. E. (2017). *A comparative analysis of active and mass shooters and events* (Doctoral dissertation). Retrieved from https://rucore.libraries.rutgers.edu/rutgers-lib/54108/

Daly, S. E. (In progress). School employees' decisions to intervene in school violence.

DeVoe, J. F., Peter, K., Noonan, M., Snyder, T. D., & Baum, K. (2005). *Indicators of school crime and safety: 2005*. Washington, DC: U.S. Departments of Education and Justice.

DuRant, R. H., Cadenhead, C., Pendergrast, R. A., Slavens, G., & Linder, C. W. (1994). Factors associated with the use of violence among urban black adolescents. *American Journal of Public Health, 84*, 612–617.

Elkind, D. (1967). Egocentrism in adolescence. *Child Development, 38*, 1023–1034.

Espelage, D., Anderman, E. M., Evanel Brown, V., Jones, A., Lane, K. L., MacMahon, S. D., Reddy, L. A., & Reynolds, C. R. (2013). Understanding and preventing violence directed against teachers: Recommendations for a national research, practice, and policy agenda. *American Psychologist, 68*(2), 75–87.

Felson, M., & Cohen, L. E. (1980). Human ecology and crime: A routine activity approach. *Human Ecology, 8*(4), 389–406.

Furby, L., & Beyth-Marom, R. (1992). Risk taking in adolescence: A decision-making perspective. *Developmental Review, 12*(1), 1–44.

Gabor, D. (1963). *Inventing the future*. London: Secker & Warburg.

Gagnon, J. C., & Leone, P. E. (2001). Alternative strategies for school violence prevention. *New Directions for Youth Development, 92*, 101–125.

Galand, B., Lecocq, C., & Philippot, P. (2007). School violence and teacher professional disengagement. *British Journal of Educational Psychology, 77*, 465–477.

Giedd, J. N., Blumenthal, J., Jeffries, N. O., Castellanos, F. X., Liu, H., Zijdenboxs, A., Paus, T., Evans, A. C., & Rapoport, J. L. (1999). *Brain development during childhood and adolescence: A longitudinal MRI study. Nature Neuroscience, 2*(10), 861–863.

Gordon, R. A., Lahey, B. B., Kawai, E., Loeber, R., Stouthamer-Loeber, M., & Farrington, D. P. (2004). Antisocial behavior and youth gang membership: Selection and socialization. *Criminology, 42*(1), 55–88.

Henderson, N., & Millstein, M. M. (2003). *Resilience in schools: Making it happen for students and educators*. Thousand Oaks, CA: Corwin Press.

Hinduja, S., & Patchin, J. W. (2017). Cultivating youth resilience to prevent bullying and cyberbullying victimization. *Child Abuse and Neglect, 73*, 51–62.

Hirschi, T. (1969 [2011]). Social bond theory. Reprinted in F. T. Cullen & R. Agnew (Eds.), *Criminology theory: Past to present* (4th ed.) (pp. 229–237). New York: Oxford University Press.

Horner, R., Sugai, G., Smolkowski, K., Todd, A., Nakasato, J., & Esperanza, J. (2009). A randomized control trial of school-wide positive behavior support in elementary schools. *Journal of Positive Behavior Interventions, 11*(3), 113–144.

Jones, S. M., Brown, J. L., Hoglund, W. L. G., & Aber, J. L. (2010). A school-randomized clinical trial of an integrated social-emotional learning and literacy intervention: Impacts after one school year. *Journal of Counseling and Clinical Psychology, 78*(6), 829–842.

Kohlberg, L. (1968). The child as a moral philosopher. *Psychology Today, 2*(4), 24–30.

Kupersmidt, J. B., & Coie, J. D. (1990). Preadolescent peer status, aggression, and school adjustment as predictors of externalizing problems in adolescence. *Child Development, 61*, 1350–1362.

LaRusso, M. D., & Aber, J. L. (2010). Improving classroom quality: Teacher influences and experimental impact of the 4Rs Program. *Journal of Educational Psychology, 102*(1), 151–167.

Marzano, R. J. (2003). *What works in schools: Translating research into action.* Alexandria, VA: Association for Supervision and Curriculum Development.

Mateu-Gelabert, P., & Lune, H. (2003). School violence: The bidirectional conflict flow between neighborhood and school. *City & Community, 2*(4), 353–368.

Merton, R. K. (1938). Social structure and anomie. *American Sociological Review, 3*(5), 672–682.

Musu-Gillette, L., Zhang, A., Wang, K., Zhang, J., & Oudekerk, B. A. (2017). *Indicators of school crime and safety: 2016* (NCES 2017-064/NCJ 250650). Washington, DC: National Center for Education Statistics, U.S. Department of Education, and Bureau of Justice Statistics, Office of Justice Programs, U.S. Department of Justice.

NAACP Legal Defense and Educational Fund. (2008). Dismantling the school-to-prison pipeline. Retrieved from http://www.naacpldf.org/.

National Crime and Victimization Survey. (n.d.). *Bureau of Justice Statistics.* Retrieved from https://www.bjs.gov/index.cfm?ty=dcdetail&iid=245.

Newman, K. S., Fox, C., Harding, D. J., Mehta, J., & Roth, W. (2005). *Rampage: The social roots of school shootings.* New York, NY: Basic.

Positive Behavioral Interventions & Supports (PBIS). (n.d.). "What Is School-Wide PBIS?" Retrieved from https://www.pbis.org/.

Reiss, A. L., Abrams, M. T., Singer, H. S., Ross, J. L., & Denckla, M. B. (1996). Brain development, gender, and IQ in children: A volumetric imaging study. *Brain, 119*(Pt. 5), 1763–74.

Romer, D., Reyna, V. F., & Satterthwaite, T. D. (2017). Beyond stereotypes of adolescent risk taking: Placing the adolescent brain in development context. *Development Cognitive Neuroscience, 27*, 19–34.

Roper v. Simmons, 543 U.S. 551. (2004). Brief for the American Psychological Association, and the Missouri Psychological Association as *Amici Curiae* Supporting Respondent.

Sandy Hook Promise. (2018). Say something training fact sheet. Retrieved from https://www.sandyhookpromise.org/block_say_something.

Skiba, R., Simmons, A. B., Peterson, R., & Forde, S. (2006). The SRS safe schools survey. A broader perspective on school violence prevention. In S. R. Jimerson & M. J. Furlong (Eds.), *The handbook of school violence and school safety: From research to practice* (pp. 157–170). Mawah, NJ: Lawrence Erlbaum Associates, Inc.

Steinberg, M. P., Allensworth, E., & Johnson, D. W. (2011). *Student and teacher safety in Chicago Public Schools.* Chicago: Consortium on Chicago School Research at the University of Chicago. Retrieved from http://ccsr.uchicago.edu/sites/default/files/publications/SAFETY%20IN%20CPS.pdf .

Sutherland, E. H., & Cressey, D. R. (1960). A theory of differential association. In F.T. Cullen & R. Agnew (Eds.), *Criminological theory: Past to Present* (122–125). Los Angeles: Roxbury Publishing.

Swain-Bradway, J., Johnson, S. L., Bradshaw, & McIntosh, K. (2017). What are the economic costs of implementing SWPBIS in comparison to the benefits from reducing suspensions? *Positive Behavioral Interventions & Supports.* Retrieved from http://www.pbis.org/Common/Cms/files/pbisresources/EconomicCostsSWPBIS.pdf.

Thornberry, T. P., Lizotte, A. J., Krohn, M. D., Farnworth, M., & Jang, S. J. (1994). Delinquent peers, beliefs, and delinquent behavior: A longitudinal test of interactional theory. *Criminology, 32*(1), 47–83.

Tyler, T. (1992). *Why people obey the law.* New Haven, CT: Yale University Press.

Vartanian, L. R. (2000). Revisiting the imaginary audience and personal fable constructs of adolescent egocentrism: A conceptual review. *Adolescence, 35*(140), 639–661.

VHSSS. (2008). *Virginia high school safety study: Descriptive report of survey results from ninth grade students and teachers.* Retrieved from https://curry.virginia.edu/uploads/resourceLibrary/vhss-ninth-grade-survey-report-7-13-08.pdf.

Vidourek, R. A., King, K. A., & Merianos, A. L. (2016). School bullying and student trauma: Fear of avoidance associated with victimization. *Journal of Prevention & Intervention in the Community, 44*(2), 121–129.

Wang, M., & Holcombe, R. (2010). Adolescents' perceptions of school environment, engagement, and academic achievement in middle school. *American Educational Research Journal, 47,* 633–662.

Warr, M. (1998). Life-course transitions and desistance from crime. *Criminology, 36*(2), 183–216.

Welsh, W. N., & Harris, P. W. (2016). *Criminal justice policy and planning: Planned change* (5th ed.). New York: Taylor & Francis.

Woodland, M. H. (2016). After-school programs: A resource for young black males and other urban youth. *Urban Education, 51*(7), 770–796.

Index

About the Author

Sarah E. Daly is an assistant professor of Criminology, Law, and Society at St. Vincent College in Latrobe, Pennsylvania. Prior to joining the faculty at the college, she taught high school Spanish in Camden County, New Jersey, for nine years before assuming the role of school counselor in the same district.

Throughout her professional career, Dr. Daly continued to enroll in graduate programs to learn more about those issues and find best practices to help her students and the district. Her current research at St. Vincent College focuses on everyday school violence such as bullying and fighting to identify ways to prepare teachers and school staff. Additionally, she studies mass shootings and large-scale violence using a developmental, psychological perspective.

She hopes that her experience in schools and the research that she conducts will help to inform school policy to prepare for, prevent, and reduce small- and large-scale school violence. Her current work studies the factors that affect school employees' decisions to intervene in physical violence. Most recently, she testified before the Pennsylvania House and Senate Education Committees about ways to improve school safety.

Dr. Daly earned her bachelor's degree from the University of Notre Dame, her school counseling degree from the University of Pennsylvania, and her master's degree and doctorate from Rutgers University–Camden and Rutgers University–Newark, respectively. She has also served as a consultant on violence for the New Jersey Education Association. At St. Vincent College, she teaches courses on school violence, mass violence, research methodology, and issues of race in the criminal justice system.

CPSIA information can be obtained
at www.ICGtesting.com
Printed in the USA
FSHW020950190719
60190FS